REINCARNATION

ILLUSION OR REALITY?

REINCARNATION

ILLUSION OR REALITY?

By

Edmond Robillard, O.P.

Translated

By

K.D. Whitehead

ALBA · HOUSE   NEW · YORK

SOCIETY OF ST. PAUL, 2187 VICTORY BLVD., STATEN ISLAND, NEW YORK 10314

Library of Congress Cataloging in Publication Data

Robillard, Edmond, 1917-
  Reincarnation, illusion or reality.

  Translation of: La réincarnation, rêve ou réalité.
  1. Christianity and reincarnation. 2. Reincarnation
—Controversial literature. I. Title.
BR115.R4R613   236   82-1638
ISBN 0-8189-0432-1   AACR2

Nihil Obstat:
James T. O'Connor, S.T.D.
Censor Librorum

Imprimatur:
Joseph T. O'Keefe
Vicar General, Archdiocese of New York
April 9, 1982

The Nihil Obstat and Imprimatur are
a declaration that a book or pamphlet is considered
to be free from doctrinal or moral error. It it is not implied
that those who have granted the Nihil Obstat and
Imprimatur agree with the contents,
opinions or statements expressed.

Designed, printed and bound in the United States of
America by the Fathers and Brothers of the
Society of St. Paul, 2187 Victory Boulevard,
Staten Island, New York 10314, as part of their
communications apostolate.

---

2 3 4 5 6 7 8 9 (Current Printing: first digit).

CONTENTS

APPENDIX

INTRODUCTION

In speaking of the immortality of the soul in his *Thoughts*, Blaise Pascal observed that there was

> "... a great difference between those who do everything possible to learn about it, and those who go on living without bothering about it or even thinking about it" (Pascal, *Pensées*, Brunschvicq Edition, Fragment 194).

The recent appearance in Quebec of so many new "Gnosticisms" that have brought the doctrine of reincarnation back into fashion—after it had once disappeared so thoroughly from Christian-oriented society—invites us to reflect anew on the nature of our Christian belief in the immortality of the soul and in the resurrection of the body.

In this book I do not intend to treat the doctrine of reincarnation in all its aspects. What I am particularly interested in, is the form the doctrine assumed in India, which, with scarcely any changes, has been promoted by theosophists and the members of other esoteric sects among us.

Nor do I intend to treat in depth the question of Gnosticism. However, it has been impossible to avoid mentioning this philosophy numerous times in the course of this work, and that for two principal reasons: first, because Gnosticism greatly influenced the doctrine of reincarnation by proposing itself as the means of liberation from the endless, evil *cycle of births*; secondly, because it is primarily through gnostic-type groups and sects that the doctrine of reincarnation is being revived among us. Since

Gnosticism, as I shall explain, claims to be able to liberate men from reincarnation, it requires that men believe that they have to be liberated from a cycle of births—so that they will accept Gnosticism's means of liberation of them from this cycle.

Finally, I would not like it to be thought that the Church is entirely without resources against today's gnostic ideas and propaganda so contrary to her most fundamental beliefs. Gnosticism, like belief in reincarnation, was widespread in the Greco-Roman world at the very time when St. Paul began his mission. Let us not therefore imagine that St. Paul's world in which astrology, magic and many strange rites abounded, was only waiting to hear about the Gospel of the resurrection in order to believe in it. On the contrary, when St. Paul, preaching before the Areopagus in Athens, raised the question of the resurrection, he was laughed at, and his hearers remarked, "We would like to hear you talk about this again" (Ac 17:32).

It was in order to prevent the diffusion of faith in the resurrection of Christ and of all men that Gnosticism arose in the first place, seeking to corrupt the doctrines of Christianity and to mislead the Christian faithful.

Gnosticism, has certainly been one of the Church's most formidable and persistent enemies. Yet on Radio Canada I heard not too long ago the following from the Grand Master of the Rosicrucians, Raymond Bernard:

> "Although I am a Catholic, I certainly could have become a nonbeliever today. But not only am I a believer, I am a fervent believer. Fervent, because the belief to which I have come by means of the meditations in which I have been trained, by means of the formation which I have been given, has been transformed into a *certitude*. . . ."

Hearing this sort of discourse, I was pained to think that any Christian could imagine that the revealed mysteries of our faith *could* be transformed into absolute certitudes based on mere rational proofs or "meditation." I realized that such as Simon Magus and Valentinus, the ancient Gnostic opposed by St. Irenaeus, were far from dead, and that we now might well expect to find some new *Treatise on the Resurrection* on our doorstep written in a way so as to deceive the unwary Christian, and in which we would find all sorts of ideas thrown out along with mention of the names of St. Paul or St. John—but in which we would *not* find the true faith of Jesus Christ, He Who died and then rose again from the dead; nor would we find faith in the bodily resurrection of those who believe and live in Him.

In fact, a few years later, I actually ran across a handsomely bound copy of *The Imitation of Christ* being distributed free to Christian audiences, the preface of which spoke almost exclusively of "esoteric doctrines," the "mysterious wisdom of Solomon" and similar questionable gnostic-type topics; in the notes of this book could be discerned a plain effort to transform such an orthodox classic as the *Imitation* into a work containing "secret" teachings on reincarnation. *Gnosticism never changes.* An opinion of Saint Augustine, who was himself a Manichean gnostic before being converted to Christianity, perfectly expresses my own opinion on the matter:

> "Mani was chiefly concerned to drown simple people in confusion. At first he would promise to throw light upon and clear up the most arduous difficulties, but he would end up by demanding blind faith even on the most doubtful points. If you ever obliged him to declare which doctrines had in fact been revealed to him, he would waver and simply order you to believe. It became impossible to tolerate such deviousness combined with such extravagant pride."

I hope that the reader will find in this book the real truth concerning the respective questions of reincarnation and the resurrection, and will then be able to form a lucid and objective judgment on these much disputed questions.

REINCARNATION

ILLUSION OR REALITY?

Originally published as *La Réincarnation, Rêve ou Réalité*, by Éditions Paulines, Montreal, 1981, and Apostolat des Éditions, Paris, 1981.

PART ONE

ORIGIN AND EVOLUTION

OF THE

DOCTRINE OF REINCARNATION

I

VARIOUS ASPECTS OF THE DOCTRINE
OF REINCARNATION

Summary. Definition of the word "reincarnation." Antiquity of the doctrine. Reincarnation as understood by the Druids; by Plato and the Platonists; by the Orphic cults. It is not true that the ancient Egyptians believed in the doctrine.

Definition of Reincarnation

Reincarnation is in no way a scientific truth; it is a *religious belief*. In its essentials, this belief can be stated as follows: after death, the human soul leaves the body and passes into another body which can be either 1) a plant body (such as a grain of wheat); or 2) an animal body (such as that of a monkey or a pig); or 3) another human body (either of a rich man or poor man); or even an extra-terrestrial body.

It is in this context that we hear of such terms as *metempsychosis* (*meta*, beyond, over, plus *empsychoun*, to animate), or transmigration of souls; *metensomatosis* (*meta* plus *somatosis*, an embodiment—a concept that Plato preferred to metempsychosis; or, finally, *palingenesis* (*palin*, again, plus *genesis*, birth or origin), or a new birth or creation. Most commonly, though, we hear the terms "regeneration" or "reincarnation."

The doctrine of reincarnation is an ancient one. It could be a corruption of the belief in the immortality of the soul that some believe constituted a kind of primitive revelation to mankind.[1] Dr. Gerard Encausse, in a book entitled *La Réincarnation* (Paris, Editions Dangles, 1968), has claimed that

> The doctrine of the transmigration of souls is not exclusive to India. It can be found throughout the world; there are many who believe in it today. Classical Greece knew the doctrine and proclaimed it from the housetops. Plato believed in it; Pindar did too; Pythagoras made it a fundamental dogma of his school . . . Our ancestors, or, rather, our predecessors on the soil of France, the ancient Celts, shared the same belief, and the Druids taught it in their schools . . . (Although Gerard Encausse's book from which this passage is quoted has already gone through 23 printings, I do not recommend the book to anybody.).

These are the sort of claims made about reincarnation in most of the books on the subject. Hence I want to make a few points about belief in it in various times and places before going on in the next chapter to treat of reincarnation as it is understood in India. It is the Indian understanding of it, of course, in which I am finally interested.

The Druids

Julius Caesar (102-44 B.C.) set down in his *Gallic Wars* this short résumé of what he believed was the teaching of the Druids on reincarnation:

> Souls do not perish, but, after death, pass into another body; thus, unconcerned with death, they [the Druids] believe this doctrine should inspire virtue (*De Bello Gallico*, VI, 14).

This text is not too precise. The German tribes of the same time, it seems, believed that when a man died in combat, his soul passed into that of his brother or neighbor, redoubling thereby the courage of the latter. Perhaps Caesar confused the doctrines of the Druids with this contemporary belief of the Germans.

The Druids properly speaking were a sacerdotal caste that had originated in Brittany. In Caesar's time, their principal center was around what is today Chartres. Their influence was uneven throughout the Celtic lands. Dion Chrysostom (A.D. 30?-116) claims that the Gallic kings could decide nothing without consulting the Druids, but we find no trace of their influence in Italy, Illyria or Asia Minor.

In Gaul, the Druids certainly exercised a priestly power, even presiding over human sacrifices; and they certainly taught a doctrine, probably esoteric, to their members.

It could be that by Caesar's time their doctrine on reincarnation, originally brought from Ireland, had begun to spread across the continent; but it is unlikely that it had spread everywhere. It left more durable traces in the British Isles, and St. Patrick was still vigorously combating it in Ireland in the fifth century.

But there is really not very much that can positively be affirmed about the belief of the Druids in reincarnation, since we are really ignorant of the full content, sources, and development of Druid beliefs.

Plato and the Platonists

We are much better informed about the conception of reincarnation that we find in Plato and the Platonists.

It is not a certainty that Plato himself was completely convinced about the reality of reincarnation. In his earliest works he reveals himself as a very prudent man, as well he ought to have been, considering that his master, Socrates, had been condemned to drink the hemlock because of his alleged impiety; and that even Alcibiades, though an adopted son of Pericles, was probably headed for the same fate if he had not escaped by betraying the Athenians. Thus we have to realize that Plato always took great pains to express respect for the religious traditions of Greece. As is true of the Upanishads, so it is also true of Plato, that it is sometimes hard to understand clearly from his writings what he himself really believes and what he does not believe, though the overall effect of what he says certainly subtly undermines traditional Greek religious beliefs from within.

The similarity of Plato's thought to that of the Upanishads—about which we will speak at greater length farther on—extends to quite a number of points. The "know thyself" which Plato makes his own certainly has a more than apparent resemblance to the special "knowledge" that the Upanishads propose to their adepts as the only solution to the problem of human destiny. Moreover, Plato does believe in the immortality of the soul; he wrote some admirable pages about it. And immortality, for the Greeks, was the attribute of divinity *par excellence*. Thus there was little difference, on the one hand, between preaching immortality and "know thyself," and, on the other hand, proposing the identity of the self and of God, as the Upanishads do in claiming to impart a superior wisdom and a special rule of life.

Whether or not it is finally true that this marked resemblance between Plato and Indian thought means that Plato is ultimately dependent upon Indian sources for his view of reincarnation, it certainly is true that Plato is the great master and inspirer of occidental thought as far as reincarnation is concerned. In the Appendix, I am including a passage from his *Timaeus* which summarizes what he has to say about it; this passage from *Timaeus* is echoed in the *Dialogue with Trypho* of the Christian apologist St. Justin which I also include in the Appendix. This work of St. Justin dates from about the year A.D. 155; in it he recounts the difficulties he had escaping from Platonism in order to achieve a truer grasp of "Christian philosophy." The pages he feels obliged to devote to the subject of reincarnation certainly bear witness to the infatuation with it that existed in his time.

We find the same phenomenon in the *Poimandres*, a Hermetic text of the first century; it translates into gnostic terms the Platonic conception of the ascent of the soul towards its full liberation, the counterpart doctrine of the descent of the soul into its bodily prison found in the text of Plato's *Timaeus*. As we read this text from the *Poimandres* attentively, we are no longer quite sure we are not reading a Hindu work:

> At the dissolution of your material body, you leave it behind to suffer corruption, and the form you then have can no longer be seen. You also abandon to the Demon your

habitual self, henceforth inactive; even your bodily senses return to their source in nature and become inseparable from nature and part of the primordial energy; the irascible and concupiscible appetites also revert to the nonrational. This is what becomes of the sensible nature that man owes to his body and which he must slough off.

In this way, man launches himself towards the heights through the various spheres of being: in the first zone, he abandons the power of growing or diminishing; in the second, the operations of malice henceforth become inoperative; in the third zone, the illusion of desire no longer prods him; in the fourth, the lust for power becomes divested of its temptation; in the fifth zone, presumption and temerity disappear; in the sixth, the illicit appetite for gain henceforth ceases to spur man on; in the seventh, lies and deceit lose their power to set traps for him (*Poimandres*, in *Corpus Hermeticum*, Vol. I, Treatise 1, Paris, les Belles-Lettres, 1945).

The interest of such a passage as this lies not only in the fact that it may be one of the sources of the Christian idea of the "seven deadly sins" (though in this Hermetic text these sins arise from the effect of the stars on man); the passage also illustrates the idea of escape from the body and that of reincarnation that were certainly in circulation at the time that St. Paul and later St. Justin were preaching the doctrine of the resurrection.[2]

Pythagoras and the Pythagoreans

But how could Plato have been in contact with Indian thinkers? Through the Pythagoreans and the adepts of the Orphic cults.

Pythagoras, a native of Samos who lived in the sixth century B.C., traveled according to his biographers among the Egyptians, Chaldeans, Persians and Hindus, finally establishing himself at Crotona in Southern Italy towards the year 530 B.C.

Those familiar with the manner in which the ancient writers expressed themselves will understand that such a mention of all the "travels" of Pythagoras is also another way of stating that he underwent the influence of the peoples mentioned; at the same time it is not to be excluded that Pythagoras did in fact visit their countries; the ancients traveled much more than we perhaps imagine.

Certainly the descriptions we have of the way of life of the Pythagoreans remind us of India and of the style of contemporary Buddhist monasteries: the Pythagorean adepts wore distinctive dress; they were rigorous vegetarians, and they even shunned certain kinds of vegetables such as beans. Finally, they believed that the soul was a prisoner in the body, that it was subject to reincarnation, and that it could only escape from the cycle of births by means of a pure and spotless life.

The doctrines of the Pythagoreans provide a source for Plato and explain the reasons for the similarity between his doctrine and theirs.

In 1917, an ancient basilica was uncovered in Rome in the Via Presnestina, near the Porta Maggiore, in which a cult was practiced that has all the characteristics of the neo-Pythagorean religion; this cult was evidently still flourishing around the time of Christ. And we can read in the *Dialogue with Trypho* of St. Justin already mentioned about the encounter that St. Justin had with the neo-Pythagoreans:

> My soul . . . was always desirous of learning the essence and principles of philosophy.
>
> I therefore went to a celebrated Pythagorean, proud of his wisdom. I expressed the desire to become his pupil and disciple.
>
> He asked me: "Have you learned astronomy, geometry, and music? Do you imagine that you can comprehend the way that leads to happiness if you have not first learned what makes it possible for the soul to become detached from the objects of the senses and become capable of appreciating spiritual realities—the contemplation of the good and the beautiful?"
>
> Then he praised again the sciences he had mentioned

which he declared were necessary prerequisites for wisdom. And he dismissed me when I admitted that I had not studied them. I was disappointed at this outcome, all the more because I greatly respected this sage. But I reflected on how much time it would take me to study all these things, and I could not reconcile myself to the idea of taking so much time" (St. Justin, *Dialogue with Trypho*, Chapter 2).

Here, again, we notice how believers in the doctrine of reincarnation propose to their followers a particular type of asceticism—in the case of the Pythagoreans, an *intellectual* asceticism—as the means by which the soul can be liberated from the body. How the first Christians must have found, in such circles as these, a resistance to their dogma of bodily resurrection!

The Orphic Cults

The tie with India is much more evident in the case of the Orphic cults. Orphism came to Greece as a religion imported from Asia—more precisely, from Thrace. It was not a state religion. Members of the Athenian elite belonged, organized in fraternities or brotherhoods that were both autonomous and "esoteric." In the eyes of the people, the members of these brotherhoods were apt to be ridiculed because of their pretentions of being especially pure or of being "saints."

Pindar and Euripides evidence a knowledge of the workings of these Orphic cults; and Plato was evidently very close to them.

The Orphic cults exhibited a belief in a *cycle of births*, or *wheel of fortune*—and these doctrines are almost certain indications of a belief in reincarnation. Souls, after having descended to Hades, came back to earth and were reborn. One important point was that there was believed to be a fixed and invariable number of souls, from which it followed that humanity could only maintain itself through this return of the souls of the dead to the world of the living. Such a conception, which I would even characterize as a metaphysical one entailing the necessity of the world, required the necessity of reincarnation as the means to conserve living species, and played a great role in Greek thought; it was a conception totally alien to the idea of *creation*, one which could not even conceive of a world which was not "necessary."

The initiates enrolled in the Orphic brotherhoods who participated in the mysteries had to undergo an expiation of their faults—or, rather, a purification from their defilements, the most serious of which was the very fact that they consisted of a body as well as a soul. Following this purification, they were supposed to be definitively "liberated" and then enter upon a "divine" existence, exactly as Hindu Brahmins are supposed to do following their *Divine Way*. Virtue thus became the door leading to an eternity of intoxication.

Orphism required of its initiates a series of continual purifications throughout their entire lives on earth. Contributing to this purification were both ascetic practice and the reading of and meditation on the Orphic books. We wonder if St. Paul was not thinking of some Orphic-type sect when he wrote the following remarkable lines (which also remind us of some of today's cults):

> . . . Why do you still let rules dictate to you, as though you were still living in the world? "It is forbidden to pick up this, it is forbidden to taste that, it is forbidden to touch something else." All these prohibitions are only concerned with things that perish by their very use—an example of human doctrines and regulations. It may be argued that true wisdom is to be found in these, with their self-imposed devotions, their self-abasement and their severe treatment of the body; but once the flesh starts to protest, they are no use at all (Col 2:20-23).

Such an asceticism, in St. Paul's eyes, accomplished nothing essential, since it was entirely conceived as liberating the soul from matter and from the endless cycle of births; thus it resembled the superficial ritual purity of the Pharisees, and was more concerned with merely having clean hands than with also having a pure heart in the true sense.

Notions of merit and demerit were also very important in the Orphic system because it was believed that the soul after death was assigned to a happy or unhappy reincarnation according to the individual's accumulated merits or demerits (the law of Karma).

Whether or not associated with the ancient Orphic cults properly speaking, the mythological figure of Orpheus himself retained its attraction in certain Christian circles. Christ and Orpheus were sometimes compared, as can be seen in a passage of Eusebius' *Panegyric of Constantine*; it is possible that some Christians hoped to bring adepts of Orphic-type belief in reincarnation to a belief in the resurrection by transforming the myth of Orpheus—and by showing Jesus surrounded by pagans reduced to the level of animals (Rm 1:20-27) as a result of their denial of the "image of God" in which they had been created.

Egyptian Religion

Gerard Encausse, whose book on reincarnation I cited above, conceived the unfortunate idea of attributing to the ancient Egyptians his own belief in reincarnation. The publishers of the twenty-third edition of his book compounded this error by reproducing on the cover an illustration from the Egyptian *Book of the Dead* which in fact teaches a doctrine wholly at variance with reincarnation.

Herodotus created a false impression in this regard, probably founded on the tradition that Pythagoras had also visited Egypt. Assuming that he did visit Egypt, he certainly did not learn anything of his reincarnation doctrine there; for the idea of reincarnation is in absolute contradiction with the conception that the ancient Egyptians had of the world to come, and with the cult that they rendered to their dead.

The *Book of the Dead* does speak of transformations that the dead may make of themselves: into falcons, lotuses, phoenixes, swallows, serpents, crocodiles, etc. But these transformations were for the purposes of escaping the perils of the next world; it was never a question of metempsychosis; these changes were voluntary and were to be produced by *magic*; they had nothing to do with punishments imposed on the dead because of bad conduct in their previous existence.

Even these magical transformations, always presumed to be

for the advantage of the dead, never played anything except a very secondary role in Egyptian religion. I find all this very well explained by a contemporary author:

> The spirit traveled to the land of the shades. According to the *Book of the Dead*, the spirit could move at will from one world to the other and avoid any dangers he might encounter in the other world. The spirit retained something of the personality of the deceased, because he fed on offerings presented by the living to that particular person, and he would come back to torment the living in case they neglected to present them.[3] But the spirit reflected the deceased's personality imperfectly; even if he accepted his share in the offerings, the latter were nevertheless not directly addressed to him.
>
> It was to the *double* of the deceased that these offerings were in fact directed. It was the double that remained the faithful companion of the body for which he had been created; he required a material support, namely, the body. Hence the necessity for embalming the latter, or, if that was not possible, for making a statue of the deceased. It was the double who conserved, in the embalmed body or in the statue, the personality of the deceased.
>
> It is easy to see that the practice of embalming, which had such an important part in Egypt because it was considered necessary for the subsistence of the double, implied a belief that simply contradicted metempsychosis (R. Hedde, *Dictionnaire de Théologie Catholique*, Article "Metempsychosis," Col. 1577-78).[4]

But there is more. Not only did the ancient Egyptians' conception of the next world forbid a belief in reincarnation; a belief in bodily resurrection actually took root among them. This can be seen in the great myth of Osiris which originated at a very early period, around 3000 B.C.; elements of this myth may have been borrowed, perhaps from the Phoenicians or Babylonians. In this myth we see appearing under Babylonian influence the god Seth, deity of shadows and of evil, who slays Osiris and scatters his members; but Isis, the sister as well as the spouse of Osiris, gathers his members back together again and brings Osiris back to life. Such a myth evidences belief in the eventual triumph of *good* over *evil*; it also evidences belief in a coming back to life, a future resurrection. In this resurrection, the double will be assured of a true, eternal beatitude. Thus did the extraordinary religious spirit of the Egyptians intuit the nature of human eschatology.

Summary

This very rapid overview of the history of the doctrine of reincarnation among some of the peoples involved in the evolution of the Western World bears witness to the antiquity of belief in reincarnation.

The whole subject will be pursued in the following chapter, as I have already indicated, with a more in-depth study of the history of the doctrine of reincarnation in India.

Franz Cumont, the author of *Lux Perpetua*, a study of the pagan religions of the Roman Empire at the time of Christ, summarizes as follows the ancient pagan conception of the human soul. The soul was a principle of survival; it was not, for the ancients, a purely spiritual entity, but rather

> . . . a diaphonous breath analogous to the wind, an impalpable shadow barely visible to the eyes, or a mixture of air and fire. Even the Platonists who proclaimed the soul's essence to be immaterial taught that it assumed a definite form once it descended from the celestial heights to penetrate our world[5] and believed that it was wrapped in an "envelope"[6] before it ever came to inhabit a body. The soul was thus not a pure spirit that escaped the limitations of space; it was impossible to say that, like the Universal Soul,[7] the soul was everywhere and nowhere at the same time. The soul traveled in the sensible world and successively inhabited parts of it. After death it was transported to a definite region of the Universe (Franz Cumont, *Lux Perpetua*, Paris, Paul Geuthner, 1949, p. 3).

Let us note here how long it took Christians to conceive of the soul as a "pure spirit." St. Thomas Aquinas, in the Middle Ages, was one of the first theologians to affirm flatly that the soul is a simple substance capable of subsisting by itself, and, at the same time—what only seems to some contradictory—that the soul is the "substantial form" of the human composite.[8]

Footnotes

1. Belief in the immortality of the soul, and its survival after death and the corruption of the body, is one of humanity's most ancient beliefs, although it is not easy to explain its origin. The *Encyclopedia Quillet* ascribes it to a "primitive revelation." It is thus an amazing thing that the ancient Hebrews did not explicitly sanction the belief until a few years before the birth of Jesus, that is to say, in the Book of Wisdom (3:9).
2. Read Text I in the Appendix.
3. I am writing this page on Halloween, and I cannot resist pointing out the resemblance to this ancient Egyptian belief of the "tricks or treats" of modern children who threaten to torment all who fail to make their food offering. This is a prime example of a pagan survival among Christians with the mascarade recalling the necessity of praying for the dead.
4. For a more recent exposé on the same subject, see Henri Frankfort, *La Royauté et les Dieux*, Paris, Payot, 1951, p. 103: "The *Ba* [double] needed the body, or, at least, the statue of the deceased in order to conserve its identity. The double was represented as joining the body in the tomb after having circulated around the fields and woods. Often the double was shown hovering over the cadaver or descending into the tomb towards the mortuary chamber."
5. We shall see that the Indians had a similar conception of the soul and attributed to it a *subtle body* that accompanied it throughout all its reincarnations.
6. We saw earlier in the *Poimandres* how the soul was supposed to rise towards its beatitude (return to its divine condition), sloughing off the "envelopes" that subjected it to the pernicious influence of the stars that caused lying, debauchery, etc.
7. The "Universal Soul" of the Stoics corresponded to the "Cosmic Energy" of the Upanishads—as it corresponds to the "cosmic energy" posited by many modern Gnostics; it is the great *All*, in which the soul will be dissolved once it becomes liberated from its subtle body.
8. Read Text II in the Appendix.

II

THE ORIGIN AND DEVELOPMENT OF THE
DOCTRINE OF REINCARNATION
IN ANCIENT INDIA

Summary. The invasion of India and the imposition of the religion of the Aryans. The religion of the indigenous Indians: 1) the practice of Yoga; 2) belief in reincarnation.

India has been the favored center of belief in reincarnation, just as Egypt was the favored center of belief in resurrection.

It is therefore understandable that I accord more importance to the Indian conception of reincarnation than to other conceptions, and this for two obvious reasons. First of all, the Indians very early described their ideas on the subject in writing, in their sacred books, and hence we need not get lost in various fruitless conjectures concerning just what their position was. Secondly, modern works on reincarnation are inspired by Indian sources to such an extent that it is only by means of constant reference to the Vedas and to their systematization in the Vedanta that we can even understand some of these modern works; thus we too must go back to the Vedas and the Vedanta.

At the outset, let us make it clear that the texts in the Rig Veda, the oldest sacred Indian writings, make no mention of reincarnation. We do not find reincarnation mentioned until we reach the Vedanta—the later parts of the Vedic writings, consisting especially of the speculative treatises called the Upanishads. In these later writings of the Vedic literature, doctrine is reinterpreted by thinkers who attempt to formulate the idea of reincarnation so that it will be compatible with the original Aryan religion on the one hand; while, on the other hand, it will still serve to help men escape from the endless cycle of births that is now assumed to be a fact.

It is thus not an original doctrine of reincarnation that the Vedanta proposes to us, but a doctrine that has been somewhat revised. Nevertheless we need not be unduly concerned about this, since an attentive reading of the Vedanta will still provide us with a sufficient idea of what the original doctrine consisted of.

For the time being, let us simply follow the relevant history of the matter without attempting to decipher every detail of it.

The Aryan Invasion and the Vedic Religion

The indigenous populations of India that were established in the Indus Valley were subjected to a series of rude shocks between about 1800 and 1000 B.C.

These dark-skinned populations were invaded by Aryan tribes of lighter color who swept down into the upper and middle Indus Valley via Kabul and Kandahar, and succeeded in establishing themselves especially in the region of the Seven Rivers. From there, after many battles, the conquerors proceeded towards the Bay of Bengal, always pushing farther south the indigenous Dravidian populations.

The wars that took place during these invasions resembled those conducted by the Moslems in that they took on the character of holy wars. The Aryans entrusted their fortunes to their god, Indra, and it was in Indra's name that they imposed their religion on the peoples that they conquered and reduced to servitude. It is possible to gain some idea of the pitiless character of their conquests from the fact that they considered the dark-skinned aborigines falling under their sway equivalent to "*dasyus,*" or demons, whose destruction was thought to please Indra. Some of the hymns of the Rig Veda transform these aborigines into monster demons, "without noses" but with three heads and six eyes. Indra is called upon to help subdue these people "without the law," that is to say, ignorant of the Vedic religion of the conquerors; and to bring them under the sway of those "who hold the sacrificial power," that is to say, the Brahmins, priests of the Aryan religion.

It is not hard to imagine the lot of these dark-skinned peoples conquered by lighter-skinned warriors who could even have been blond. Suppressed in their deepest aspirations, the indigenous Davidian populations were obliged to keep silent and to keep their distance, nourishing the desire of revenge in their hearts.

The Religion of the Aryans

The religion that the Aryans imposed upon India was not dissimilar to the pagan religion found in Athens and in Rome around the beginning of the Christian era.

The primordial act of this pagan religion was *sacrifice*, an offering made to the Divinity in return for which the one performing the sacrifice might hope for divine beneficence and assistance.

The sacrifice normally consisted of an offering of cereals, milk, butter and the like thrown into a fire, while another portion of the same food was consumed. It was believed that the part of the food that was burned rose up to appease the god, while the part consumed testified to an intimate communion with the divine during which one literally sat and feasted at a god's table.

In the beginning, these sacrifices were probably offered by individuals, as was the case in Israel before the establishment of the Temple. As time passed, however, a caste of Brahmins, or priests, began to specialize in the offering of the sacrifices and in the regulating of the religious life of the people generally. Observances became more and more complicated; eventually it became practically impossible for individuals to offer valid sacrifices without the help of the priestly caste, since the Brahmins alone knew the sacred text and the hymns and the other appropriate matter for each kind of sacrifice.

Parallel with the establishment of the sacerdotal Brahmin caste, there appeared three other castes: the *Kshatriva*, or warrior caste, the task of whose members was to protect the people by force of arms; and the *Vaisya* caste, the members of which were responsible for commerce, agriculture, animal husbandry, etc. Finally, there was the *Sudra* caste, consisting of descendants of the conquered indigenous populations, who were supposed to serve the three higher classes as laborers or artisans; a member of this Sudra caste was, in effect, a pariah who remained outside the system of caste privileges.

Regarding the fundamental beliefs and practices of the Aryan religion, it is possible to summarize as follows: 1) there was a cult of *Brahman*, creator and organizer of the world, consisting of the recitation of hymns and of the teaching of myths about creation and retribution; 2) a cult of *ancestors*, requiring offerings of food and water, offerings which made it possible for the shades of ancestors to enter into an "ancestral heaven"; 3) a cult of *lesser gods* and spirits (Bhutas), requiring the sacrifice of animals or simply of grain or rice; and 4) a cult of *men* enjoining hospitality to Aryans, especially to Brahmins!

Generally speaking, the problem of survival after death was treated as follows in the Aryan religion: those who led a morally good life entered the "ancestral heaven" already mentioned; those whose lives were morally bad were cast into an "outer darkness"—if we may thus express the Aryan concept with a biblical phrase. All in all, though, the early Vedic writings are quite vague on the subject of retribution; the Indians did not have the facility that the Greeks had for describing Tartarus or the tortures of the damned in the next world.

In summary, we can say that the religion of the Aryans was not dissimilar to that of the Pygmies (if the light-skinned Aryans will pardon the comparison!). There was an omniscient and all-powerful god, Indra, who granted to his followers a just recompense or a deserved punishment for their good or evil actions during the course of their earthly lives. In this original Aryan religion, there was no reincarnation, only eternal retribution, or reward and punishment.

The religion of the Indigenous Indians

Long before the Aryan invasions, the indigenous Indians had

developed their own religious systems. Although long suppressed by the violent impositions of the Aryan masters, features of these indigenous systems eventually not only resurfaced but even came to dominate thought within the framework of the later official Hindu religion. It would be impossible to explain either the veritable religious revolution attested to by the Upanishads, or, indeed, the appearance of Buddhism, without reference to a resurgence of these ancient indigenous Indian beliefs, for both Buddhism and the Upanishads represent a reappearance and modification of the indigenous Indian religion. In considering these religious revolutions we must try to trace their antecedents in the history of two fundamental features of the original indigenous Indian religion: 1) Yoga; and 2) belief in reincarnation.

1. Yoga

The practice of Yoga goes back to a very ancient period in the history of India. On this point, I cite the article in the *New Catholic Encyclopedia*:

> The doctrine and practice of Yoga go back to a much earlier period than the texts, perhaps to the very beginning of Indian culture. A figure in the characteristic posture of a yogi was found among the excavations at Mohenjo-Daro, Pakistan, where the remains date from the 2nd millenium B.C. In any case, it is probable that Yoga originated among the pre-Aryan peoples of India and has its roots in certain mystical and magical traditions of a very primitive character.
>
> The decisive development of Yoga took place in about the 6th century B.C. when an ascetical movement arose, perhaps as a result of the doctrine of transmigration of souls, which seems to have entered into Hindu tradition at this time. This ascetical movement was to have a permanent effect on Indian culture, for from it Buddhism and Jainism were born, and the doctrine of the Upanishads took shape under its influence (B. Griffiths, "Yoga," *The New Catholic Encyclopedia*, 1967, vol. 14, p. 1071).

The second part of this text deserves close analysis. Yoga

existed before the Aryan invasions. From the beginning it had its own aims and purposes. Only later did it come to appear as an essential method of liberation for those wishing to escape from the cycle of births.

Yoga was born out of natural experiences in a context of both magic and mysticism.

The aim of Yoga was to achieve a certain state of ecstasy, or, more precisely, of *enstasy*, in which the subject escapes from the consciousness of life outside himself and, to use the Indians' own language, attains to a condition of semi-sleep, or a dreamlike state entailing complete lethargy, if I may so express myself.

The result obtained by Yoga, if I may be pardoned the comparison resembles the state of hibernating mammals in those countries where deep snow makes it impossible to forage for food during long winter months. Or again: breathing techniques, when they aim to augment significantly the quantity of oxygen inhaled by the organism, can actually procure the same state of euphoria that pilots of supersonic jetplanes experience if they inhale more oxygen than necessary.

Regardless of how these breathing techniques were actually managed, in Yoga they did aim at a religious end, and, in that respect, have to be considered alongside other religious practices that were widespread among ancient peoples.

The desire to escape from the reality that surrounds us and, thereby, it is believed, move closer to the Divinity, is one of the most universal of human desires.

In Siberia, as among certain American Indian tribes where Shamanism flourishes, divine communion is sought through dances carried on to the point of exhaustion. In ancient Israel, certain prophets flagellated and mutilated themselves in order to achieve visions and enter into contact with the divine (1 Samuel 19:20-24). The same result is sometimes sought through sexual means, as is the case today with tantric Yoga.

Recourse to alcoholic beverages and hallucinogens serves the same ends. In the course of His crucifixion, Jesus Himself was offered a beverage to attenuate His suffering, but He refused to drink it. The ancient Indians similarly knew an intoxicating drink called *soma*, concocted from a marsh plant called *indu*; the characteristics of this drink can be gathered from the hymns in its honor contained in the Rig Veda. (See Appendix III)

Thus was Yoga, in the beginning: a method of escaping from this world and of attaining communion with the divine spirit believed to inhabit the heart of the world, and indeed, the heart of man.

In order to understand a similar quest much closer to us, let us recall the search for visions described by the young Arthur Rimbaud in his poem, "Seven-Year-Old Poets":

> . . . stupid, slow, he always tried,
> To shut himself up in the cool latrine;
> There he could think, be calm, and sniff the air.
> Washed from the smells of day, the garden in winter,
> Out behind the house filled with moonlight;
> Stretched below a wall, and rolled in dirt,
> Squeezing his dazzled eyes to make the visions come....

Arthur Rimbaud too, in thus sniffing his fetid odors and crushing his eyes with his fist "to make the visions come," similarly hoped to attain to another mystical world from which life would be "absent." We can also read in his poem, "The Sister of Charity," how this adolescent poet, filled with disgust, seeks to escape from the world through the Muse, the Woman, the Revolution, Science and Death:

> The youth before the squalor of the world
> Feels his heart moved with a profound ire—
> Pierced with the deep eternal wound,
> His Sister of Charity is all his desire.
> (Arthur Rimbaud, *Complete Works*. Translated from the French by Paul Schmidt. New York, Harper, 1975, pp. 78 and 75).

The particular "sister of charity" that India, ultimately frightened by the specter of reincarnation, sought as a blessed escape, turned out to be nothing else than Yoga, another form of Gnosticism.

In a book entitled *Death of a Guru*,[9] Rabindranath R. Maharaj, trained by his mother and father from childhood in transcendental meditation (mantra Yoga), tells how as a medical student in London, he discovered the astonishing similarity between the effects of his Yoga and those of LSD:

> I met an increasing number of those on drugs and I made a disconcerting discovery: some of them obtained from their narcotics the same experiences I achieved by means of Yoga and transcendental meditation.[10]
>
> I listened with surprise to their descriptions of the beautiful and peaceful world to which LSD had introduced them: the world of psychedelic visions with which I was only too familiar. Certainly some of them had experienced "bad trips" through their use of drugs, but the majority of these addicts were no more eager to heed these kinds of warnings than I was at the time that I was practicing Yoga.

We have to add, though, that the ancient Indians early perceived the dangers of trying to escape from the world by means of dreams and hallucinations. In the beginning, basking in the dreams induced by their techniques, they experienced a feeling of creativity and power; as an author of one of the Upanishads wrote: "He who dreams can at will build castles or conquer empires." But there was also a perception that this sort of dreaming was not always beneficent or happy in its results. The dreams could become nightmares; the "trips" could become bad trips. It was for this reason that the ancient Indians sought to perfect their techniques in order to achieve, by means of Yoga, what they called a "perfect sleep," that is to say, a total unconsciousness beyond dreams. They even saw in this latter state the beginning of nirvana, or the perfect liberation of the soul from the prison of the body and from the cycle of births.

Such was, roughly, the history of the autonomous evolution of Yoga up to the moment when it encountered the doctrine of reincarnation—about which we must now speak more directly.[11]

2. Reincarnation

How could human beings ever come to believe that the human soul, taking leave of the body, could actually pass into other bodies and take on a new existence in them?

Would it not have been more simple to believe that everything ends with death, as Pascal gives us to understand in one of his *Thoughts* that is often quoted? Thus:

> The last act is bloody, however beautiful the play may have been up to then; in the end, the grave is filled up with earth and that is the end (Pascal, *Pensées*, Brunschvicq Edition, Fragment 210).

Certainly, in recent centuries, metaphysicians have been able to demonstrate that the soul is a perfectly simple substance and hence an incorruptible one; but how did primitive peoples in the remotest antiquity arrive at this conclusion? How were they able to persuade themselves that there was something in man that eluded corruption?

One of the ways this belief undoubtedly came about was through the nearly universal human experience of *"possession,"* or the taking over, however temporarily, of people's personalities by alien souls or spirits. On the simplest level we need think only of such examples of this as the husband who is completely devoted to his wife but who suddenly and inexplicably abandons her; as the sober, steady, peaceful kind of man who becomes a belligerent trouble-maker when he gets drunk; as the ruthless and arrogant kind of man who becomes tender and sentimental when he has imbibed too much; or as the usually timid and taciturn type of person who suddenly stands up and begins to harangue a meeting. How better explain these sudden and inexplicable kinds of personality changes than by imagining that some alien spirit has somehow taken possession of a person and brought them about?

Among the ancient Germans, as I have already noted, it was believed that when a soldier fell in battle, a brother or neighbor received his spirit and a redoubling of courage along with it. Was this a way of expressing the common experience that the anger that went along with fighting could make a man truly terrible?

Another one of the ways that the human soul came to be considered incorruptible was the *resemblance* that sometimes occurred between children and their deceased ancestors. Seeing the uncanny reflection of a person's gestures and attitudes reborn in a descendant could lead quite naturally to the belief that the ancestor was literally reborn in that descendant. Here we should take note of the tribal taboo that forbade giving to a child the name of any living relative; in the tribal mind, the identity of the name implied the identity of the person; and it was therefore believed that one of two persons bearing the same name would have to die.

Then when we take note of the importance accorded to sleep and dreams in ancient Indian religious literature, we see how it could have been from careful observation of phenomena as mysterious as *dreams* that the Indians arrived at the idea of a possible reincarnation of the soul after death.

Thus there is the man himself who sleeps; he often dreams, and, in his dreams, he can have two types of mysterious experiences of his own: 1) he can meet in his dreams with persons who have passed away, such as his mother or father, and the latter may even continue to talk with him, giving the same advice or warnings as they did when they were alive; or 2) the dreamer can himself be transported to faraway places, or be transformed into a bird or fish, or relive events of his childhood, or, on the other hand, even seem to be prematurely aged and infirm. How could anyone fail to be impressed by such dream experiences? Nothing could be more natural, confronted with them, than to conclude that: 1) the dead continue to exist in a beyond where we continue to have access to them in dreams, and where, perhaps, we can even travel to join them; 2) our spirits can leave our bodies, and, during sleep, travel independently at will, not only to faraway places but back and forth in time—and, indeed, from one body to another. Let us not forget in this connection what I said about drug use in ancient societies—this could multiply the power of dreams or hallucinations:

> Drink pulls me up like a swift team of horses drawing a chariot . . . As a whole the two great worlds do not amount to more than I do by myself . . . I have exceeded the grandeur of both heaven and earth . . . I stand with one foot in heaven already, the other on earth . . . I am great, great . . . See how I am carried up to the clouds. Should I then have drunk soma? (Rig Veda, 9.119).

How easy and natural it would have been to imagine that, during such "trips," the soul really did leave the body to achieve self-realization in numerous new ways?

Finally, we have to consider the most fundamental experience of all in the context of belief in reincarnation, namely, the experience of death. Who has not made the comparison between sleep and death? Why should death not present us with the same sorts of experiences as sleep? Why would the soul not then be able to obtain the same kind of fancy and freedom that are currently possible to us only in dreams? Shakespeare's Hamlet, at the moment when he is tempted by suicide, dwells on the thought that death is perhaps a sleep with its own kind of "dreams:"

> To die—to sleep.
> To sleep—perchance to dream: ay, there's the rub!
> For in that sleep of death what dreams may come
> When we have shuffled off this mortal coil,
> Must give us pause . . . (Shakespeare, *Hamlet*, III, I).

Others have reasoned themselves to different conclusions than Hamlet's on this subject. They have preferred the uncertainty of reincarnation to the certainty of the idea of everything ending with death and corruption in the earth; and hence they have hitched their wagons to the star of reincarnation as the vehicle that will carry their hopes of immortality.

Such are the ways, as nearly as we can conjecture, that both the doctrine of reincarnation and the practice of Yoga made their way among the ancient indigenous Indians, separately at first but eventually developing along parallel lines. At first the doctrine of reincarnation gives hope and comfort at the thought of the immortality that it confers; later on, when it is this very immortality that comes to be seen as the worst of calamities, Yoga arrives to assume the role of the unique liberator of human souls subjected to the cycle of births.

However, in order to arrive at this point, both Yoga and the doctrine of reincarnation had to undergo a long development.[12]

Footnotes

9. Published by G.R. Welch Co., Ltd., Canada, 1977, p. 168.
10. Transcendental meditation, as taught in Canada, and particularly, in Montreal by Marharishi Mahesh Yogi, is nothing else than one of the multiple forms of Yoga, namely, mantra Yoga, in which the state of *enstasy* is sought by means of repetition of verses from the Vedas; this kind of repetition acts in the manner of a hypnotic, or fixation on an object.
11. Read Text III in the Appendix.
12. Read Text IV in the Appendix.

III

THE MEETING OF THE DOCTRINE OF RE-INCARNATION WITH THE VEDIC RELIGION

Summary. Fusion of the Aryan and Indian systems: a new conception of reincarnation. The reinforcement of morality; the Indian decalogue; Indian asceticism.

A New Conception of Retribution

We do not know precisely when and under what conditions the doctrine espoused by the votaries of reincarnation was fused with the Vedic theology of retribution, or reward and punishment. However, the fusion of the two doctrines left such clear indications in the Vedic writings that we cannot doubt that the fusion took place.

Did believers in reincarnation hold at first for the existence of a unique God responsible for the conditions in which reincarnation took place? We do not know. We do not even know whether, at first, there was thought to be any relationship between the moral conduct of the soul in its previous existence and its reincarnation in either happy or unhappy circumstances.

What we do know is that the original Vedic religion did have a very well-developed eschatology. It was believed that, according to the judgment of Indra, those who did good were called after death to taste an unalloyed happiness in the luminous realms of the moon, while those whose conduct during life was evil inherited a miserable existence in a realm of shadows. (This is the typical conception of, for example, primitive African religions, which nevertheless also hold that reincarnation is sometimes possible in the case of a soul which returns to help those near and dear.)

With time, however, the picture became more complicated. Those who did good in life were still accorded an unalloyed happiness on the moon, but this happiness was only for a time, at the end of which the soul would be reincarnated in conditions that were pleasant and agreeable, in accordance with the good soul's previous merit. Those of evil conduct underwent a series of punishments in the next world, after which they too were reincarnated in conditions more or less miserable, in accordance with the demerits they had accumulated. It is this system of rewards and punishments for good or bad conduct that unmistakably testifies to the fusion of the two different religious systems: the Aryan system, and the belief in reincarnation.

Let us note in passing an interesting point. In the new fused system, the Brahmins, as priests and theologians, take care to reserve for themselves a privileged position. Was this for the purpose of maintaining Aryan supremacy? In the beginning, the Rig Veda knew only the so-named *Pitryana* for the deceased: the Way of Ancestors, ending in a paradise of light, the "ancestral heaven." To this the Brahmins added the *Devayana*, or Divine Way, reserved for the fervent elite. Those who follow the second path, it was believed, find not only an ideal happiness in the company of their ancestors; they also escape from the law of reincarnation. Once established in the Divine Way, in effect, there is no return to the endless cycle; instead one enters into the Brahman, that is to say, God; and the soul, finally divested of its subtle body, loses itself in the Brahman forever. We get the distinct impression at this point that we are witnessing the beginning of speculation about the doctrine of nirvana, for the doctrine of the Upanishads, like Buddhism, denying the existence of a transcendent God, only have to be modified at a single point in order to make possible the descent of man into his deepest self on the model of a Brahmin losing himself in the Brahman.

The Reinforcement of Morality

It is probable that at the time of the fusion of the doctrine of reincarnation with the original Vedic religion the former contributed to a marked reinforcement of morality. If ·a happy reincarnation was the reward for good conduct, and an unhappy reincarnation the punishment for bad conduct, there arose an urgent necessity to spell out more clearly what constituted good and bad conduct.

At this point, the Indian thinkers found themselves on delicate ground. In marked contrast to the Hebrews who very early had a clear idea of sin as rebellion against the God of the Covenant, the Indians were scarcely able to get past the notion of sin as merely an error or mistake; in this they resembled the Greeks, and, indeed, the majority of pagans down to our own day. Like primitive peoples, they understood the notions of pure and impure, and they also had taboos; but they never arrived at the idea that God required a certain standard of conduct from humans and was offended by their failure to measure up to His requirements.

This impression, unresolved to this day within the reincarnational system, entails very serious consequences. Man's entire destiny is tied up with his moral conduct. Jesus, for example, clearly laid down the conditions for salvation, summing them up as love of God and neighbor. Reincarnational beliefs have never achieved the same clarity—except those that attempt an illusory fusion between the doctrine of reincarnation and Christianity.

The Indian Decalogue

The Indian moral code is conceived in terms of what is called *dharma*. Dharma is based on the fact that laws exist and that one must respect them. When laws are not respected, the result is called *adharma*, or disorder.

In concrete terms, dharma has reference to what accords with the nature of every being. It is the dharma, or nature, of the serpent to bite, as it is that of the thief to steal. If the serpent ceased to bite or the thief to steal, the world would return to a primal chaos and nothing would any longer be intelligible. This view of things reminds us of that of the Greeks who were so insistent upon the importance of their *logos*, or principle of order.

The only evil in this conception of things is to go against nature. The dharma of a demon, for example, is what characterizes him as a type of being and obliges him as an individual. He can deny his own nature, and fail to carry out his obligations, but in so doing he becomes the source of a conflict that has to be resolved in some fashion if the universe is to continue. Reincarnation and its system of retribution thus serve to reestablish the equilibrium of an order that has been violated.

What, then, does the Indian ethic amount to? I do not here refer to dietary regimes (abstinence from meat or other foods), nor to the laws of pure and impure, nor to any religious observances. I limit myself only to those features that resemble the Judeo-Christian decalogue. In fact, we must distinguish between two different Indian codes, one very early, and another one somewhat later.

According to the most ancient code, men are supposed to cultivate the virtues of nonviolence, honesty, purity, good will, mercy and patience. According to the later code, they must cultivate nonviolence, honesty, purity, respect for property, charity, indulgence for the faults of others, moderation, tranquility, generosity and asceticism.

Regarding the development of this moral code, specialists are in disagreement. The scholar Max Müller, for example, believes in a degeneration of Indian morality from an authentically moral conception of sin such as can be found in the *Hymns to Varuna*. This authentic conception degenerated to a purely physical conception of sin equating it with ritual impurity. Other specialists, though, believe that there has been an inverse development. A physical, ritual conception of sin has developed into a moral one such as can be found in the Bhakti movement, where sin becomes identified with disobedience to God.

Indian Asceticism

Let us underline two characteristic tendencies of Indian morality. Where the original Aryan religion has been most influential, we find great importance placed upon cultic observances and everything connected with them; in this context, good actions are especially those which favor prayer, sacrifices, and the study of the sacred writings; the greatest crimes, on the other hand, are the actions which militate against these cultic observances. We saw when treating the question of retribution that this tendency is especially strong among the Brahmins following the Divine Way. In other Indian milieus, we find that, in accordance with the original indegenous religion, greater emphasis is placed upon the dharma and on the moral requirements of the two Indian codes, both the earlier and the later.

Let us make clear, in concluding this chapter, that Indian asceticism cannot be understood in exactly the same context as Christian asceticism. The word employed in India for asceticism is *tapas* which literally means "warmth." In the early days of the development of Indian asceticism, adepts concentrated on acquiring, particularly by means of the practice of Yoga, an interior warmth that would in turn make it possible to enjoy certain magic powers: levitation, the capacity to cause or calm storms, to call down rains, etc. During the first period of the religious revolution wrought by the Upanishads, though, the emphasis in these writings was placed upon concentration and meditation, and upon the means to realize the mystic union between the Self and the Divine which effected liberation from the cycle of births; no particular morality or moral code was a necessary corollary of this kind of emphasis.

Later on, however, there arose a debate among religious thinkers that reflected the similar conflict that raged between Christians during the debate over salvation by faith versus salvation by works. The *Brihad Aramyaka Upanishad* takes the position that asceticism does not liberate from the reincarnational cycle, while the *Chandogya Upanishad* espouses the contrary position that asceticism can accomplish such a liberation. For one school of thought, knowledge (and hence Gnosticism) suffices; for the other school of thought, asceticism and good works are required.[13]

Footnotes

13. Read Text V in the Appendix.

IV

THE UPANISHAD REVOLUTION AND
THE TRIUMPH OF THE YOGIST SOLUTION

Summary. The appearance of religious skepticism. The personal god changes into a god of "cosmic energy." Hence a new conception of retribution: the law of Karma. Some characteristics of Karma. A tardy correction of the doctrine of Karma: the Bhakti movement.

With the appearance of the Upanishads in India, we have the impression of witnessing a revolution of the same nature as the one that took place in the seventeenth and eighteenth centuries with the advent of the philosophy of the Enlightenment. Everywhere traditional religion is assailed, and skepticism undermines ancestral beliefs; a new vision of the human condition manifests itself that is no longer that of the Brahmins or "churchmen" alone, but, rather, that of the nobles of the Kshatriya or warrior caste, who are now seen to have taken up questions of culture and philosophy.

One sign of the revolution that was taking place can be seen in accounts of Brahmins coming to be instructed in religious matters by men belonging to the caste of the Kshtriyas. Another sign of the same revolution is the appearance of Buddha; having found among the Brahmins only a preoccupation with complicated and involved doctrines, Buddha reproached them by saying, "You are not concerned with whether men become better or not!" Such signs as these evidenced a veritable revolution of lay people against an unworthy clergy; it is highly significant that the Buddhist and Upanishad revolutions were contemporaneous.

Among the new religious thinkers who would produce the Upanishads, there were to be found both Voltaires, that is, rationalists and skeptics, and Rousseaus, who though perhaps romantic-type mystics themselves, were equally destructive of existing religion and, indeed, of the existing social order. With these new thinkers, we witness the birth of a body of literature, the Upanishads, similar to that which at the time of Jesus, inspired the cult of Gnosticism.

As far as this Upanishad revolution is concerned, we are particularly interested in how the doctrine of reincarnation was handled.

The Personal God Becomes a God of "Cosmic Energy"

The original Vedic religion celebrated God as a personal being responsible for the ongoing operation of the world. It would have been possible for this religion to have evolved towards the conception of one God and to have gradually come to view the other gods as diverse attributes of the one omniscient and all-powerful God. I will cite only one passage from a hymn found in the ancient Rig Veda to illustrate this conception:

> He is our father, who creates and orders and knows all creatures and conditions; he alone is able to confer on the gods their names, and all creatures learn from him (Rig Veda 10.82).

But we must notice the skepticism already manifesting itself in another text of the Rig Veda (10:29):

> This creation, whatever it emanates from, whether it has been made or whether it has not, certainly it must be said of it that the one who watches over it from the heights of heaven knows it intimately: or perhaps he does not know it?" (*The Vedas*, Marabout University, No. 146, p. 497).

A later Buddhist text is much more incisive on the same point:

The world is in such disorder. Why does Brahma not intervene? If he is indeed the master of the whole world, Brahma, the lord of all the multitudes that have been born, why did he decree the misfortune of the whole universe? Why does he not rescue the world for happiness? Why did he make a world in which there reign deception (maya), lies, excesses, and injustice (adhamma)? . . . The lord of all beings is unjust. Order (dhamma) exists, but instead he has decreed disorder (adhamma) (*Bhuridetta Jataka*, No. 543, v. 153c).

These are considerations which finally brought about the denial of a personal God; they remind us of the discussions about Providence that, in Enlightenment France, followed the great Lisbon earthquake of November 1, 1755. But we must glimpse the Rousseauist, mystical facets of the Indian religious debate as well. We can discern in the text that follows a critique of the old Vedic belief in offerings and sacrifices, and, at the same time, we can see the new belief in reincarnation appearing:

They proceed in ignorance, they [the Brahmins] who believe themselves wise and learned . . . Imagining that offerings and sacrifices are the important things, they are so far out of things they do not even imagine anything else. After having benefited from the fruits of their good works carried out beneath the celestial vault [Vedism], they come back to this world or descend to an even lower one [reincarnation].

However, to what he considers an outdated Brahmin vision, this "Rousseauist" author opposes a new, "Enlightenment"-type philosophy:

Learn the truth. Just as thousands of sparks of the same kind leap out of a dancing flame, so, my dear, do the diverse creatures come from the Imperishable—and return to him . . . He is the one who subsists in all beings as an interior soul.[14] Each being is all these things: act, asceticism, Brahman, supreme immortality. The person who understands all this in his heart of hearts is the one who here and now cuts the knot of ignorance, my dear (*Mundaka* Upanishad, I.2.8 and 10; and II.1-9-8).

Here again is evidenced another victory of indigenous Indian thought. For the Indra of the Aryan conquerors there has been substituted a *Par japati*, or "Lord of Lords," conceived as the wielder of a magical kind of power that sustains the universe (Brahmanapasthi). This god is the god of Yoga: a sort of cosmic energy that is present in everything and which can be appropriated to oneself by means of a properly directed asceticism. In this conception, a creator God who is distinct from the world is replaced by a deity identified with the world and, in particular, with the soul of each living thing.

The scientist Jean Rostand has told us what to think of this kind of monism that reduces everything to one principle of being and that turns out to lie at the heart of both the Indian and gnostic systems:

> I can only see a nuance between a monism styled "materialist" and a monism designated "spiritualist:" whether we call everything matter, or whether we call it spirit, amounts in the end to pretty much the same thing (*Ce Que Je Crois*, p. 51).

In reality, even though it might masquerade as "religion," such a monism really entails the destruction of all religion. For faith in a transcendent God, there is substituted "knowledge;" for the "I believe in God the Father almighty" of the Creed, there is substituted the "know thyself" of philosophy. The great discovery or fundamental intuition of the Upanishad revolution is the belief that the Self (Atman) is divine (Brahman). Whoever finally arrives at that position really has no further use for religious observances, morality, beliefs, or what have you: he has already acquired the key to existence:

> Now this Atman [the divine Self in each person] cannot be apprehended by means of doctrines, or of sacrifices, or of

arduous study.[15] Only he apprehends it who wills to do so: it is this Atman that reveals its own nature.

This Atman cannot be apprehended by a man who lacks the strength, nor by means of loss of consciousness, nor by means of an inadequate asceticism. But he who makes the effort to apprehend it by these means [transcendental meditation, asceticism], if he is truly wise, his Atman will enter into the sphere of Brahman.[16]

Seers, having attained to all this fully, satisfied with their knowledge, their Atman realized,[17] their passions calmed, their senses appeased, having attained Him who goes everywhere, wise, their spirits ordered—such as these truly penetrate the All (*Mundaka Upanishad* III.2.4 and 5).

Here we encounter once more the program of Gnosticism, as it was set forth in the ancient systems of such as Valentinus or the second century Alexandrian theologian Basilides; or as it is found in modern day transcendental meditation or in other similar modern Gnosticisms. The goal of every life, after the rejection of all religious practice, and, finally, of all morality,[18] is to attain by sheer force of concentration to the experience of the identity of the Self and of God, of the Atman and the Brahman. Mysticism thus kills morality, instead of integrating it into its system; the rationalism of a Voltaire gives way before the sentimentalism of a Rousseau.

The Law of Karma

Every alteration concerning the knowledge of God on the doctrinal or dogmatic plane also has implications for the moral plane. It certainly could not have been different for the religious revolution inspired by the Upanishads which replaced the notion of a transcendent God with one of an impersonal deity inextricably bound up with the world as its vital energy.

Since retribution was a major point of the doctrine of reincarnation, we now have to examine what became of the idea of retribution in the absence of a God Who is the judge of "the living and the dead."

However, in order to examine this question more accurately, let us go back a bit to get a better perspective on the whole question.

The formidable problem of the existence of evil in the world was the problem that brought in its train the transformation of the traditional Indian faith by the Upanishad revolution; we shall see this even better later on. But the point was reached where it was no longer possible to understand how evil could be attributed to a God, Indra, who was otherwise represented as both good and all-powerful: "if God wills evil, He is not good; if He does not will it yet makes no move to prevent it, it must be because He does not have the power to prevent it. In conclusion, God is neither good nor all-powerful; indeed, He does not exist at all." Thus the reasoning went.

The same questions were raised at about the same time in ancient Israel, as the Book of Job attests. Seeing the afflictions raining down upon her husband, Job's wife tells him:

> "Do you still mean to persist in your blamelessness? Curse God and die" (Jb 2:9-10).

Similarly, as the Psalmist tells us, the unbeliever, drowning in the vision of the inequality of the human condition and the veritable ocean of evils that submerge mankind, cries out:

> "There is no God" (Ps 14:1).

In India, the same question became crucial. Believers in reincarnation were impelled to flesh out an elaborate philosophical framework for what had originally been a very vague concept of rebirth mostly in order to justify the existence of evil in the world. They tried to explain the unhappy condition of humanity by postulating a previous existence in which men had sinned and hence merited their unhappiness in this existence. Evil, instead of being ascribed to God, was ascribed to man.

But this solution, although it seemed at first to salvage God's honor in the matter, raised other questions. For example: "How did the whole unhappy chain begin in the first place?" "How"—to touch upon a point of especial sensitivity today—"did it come about that two sexes were created, and women condemned to a condition inferior to that of men?" (Here we may recall that Plato, in a work I have cited, imagined in response to the same question that the Demiurge had at first created only males, but that certain ones of them had yielded to their passions and hence were reincarnated in female bodies.)

However, the idea accepted by most of antiquity of an eternal world that had always existed did not easily square with the idea of any "beginning" whatever, and hence speculations of this nature did not proceed very far.

Instead two basic ideas were reiterated: that there was a reincarnation and that there was also a retribution. Beyond these two basic ideas there were attempts to explain the mechanism of reincarnation without reference to the official religion and its sacrifices for the dead, and these attempts thus amounted to a kind of rebellion against the official religion. In this new context, retribution, or reward and punishment, became strictly an affair of pure, objective justice, regulated entirely by the law of Karma according to one's merits or demerits. It has been held that the discovery of this law provided the most complete possible solution to the problem of theodicy, of justifying the existence of evil in the world and the ways of God to man. We must examine this idea carefully.

It was believed that when the soul leaves the body it carries with it, wrapped up in the subtle body that accompanies it, the *seeds* of its future reincarnation. Past actions, both good and bad, are conserved in the soul's subtle body, and *spontaneously* give rise to their appropriate fruits in the new existence of the reincarnated individual. God is thus not necessary to the conditions of the soul's new existence. Instead a kind of impersonal but infallible organizer or "programmer" moves the soul to the new body in which the soul will either be rewarded for its predominantly good actions, or punished for its predominantly evil ones, according to the law of Karma. No priest, no sacrifice, no absolution could thus modify the fatal and irrevocable course of this order of things. No one should question why he is born a pariah, or born black: the law of Karma explains everything. Everyone is responsible for his own destiny, and whatever it is, is just.

Whoever might want to better his sutuation need do only one thing: live right. But what does "living right" actually entail? How can the errors or mistakes which have placed one in a perhaps unhappy condition be avoided? These questions are never clearly answered.

Moreover, from inside the closed circle of the law of Karma, no issue is really possible. Whoever does good will invariably be reincarnated in order to receive the reward for the good that he does. Whoever does evil will similarly be reincarnated in order to receive the punishment for the evil that he does. There is no deliverance from the cycle of births, or wheel of fortune—no delivery, that is, except Gnosticism, or the discovery of the identity of the Self and God.

Some Characteristics of Karma

It is important to describe some of the characteristics of Karma and of its pitiless law, if only to persuade imprudent Christians from too easily seeking in this kind of concept the solution to present difficulties they may feel or to evils they may experience.

The concept of Karma has very definite characteristics. First of all, one's Karma can pass from one person to another. I myself have never been able to understand how this could be the case; nevertheless it is universally understood to be the case; and this point is of great consequence. One illustration will suffice. I know a young French Canadian girl who accompanied the famous Maharishi Mahesh Yogi on a trip in the Himalayas. She witnessed a scene where a mother approached the great seer and pleaded with him to employ his powers to cure her sick child. Maharishi told her that he neither could nor would do anything for her child, since these sufferings resulted from the child's Karma, and Maharishi did not want to take this Karma upon himself. It is hardly necessary to add how such a doctrine affects our idea of charity and mutual help among men.

Furthermore, it is significant that the gods themselves are seen as subject to the law of Karma. Thus Karma is, in this respect, equivalent to the ancient Greek idea of fatality (moire), which, according to Homer, even the gods of Olympus cannot escape. The consequences of such an idea, among a people as religious as the Indians, are that prayers and offerings to the gods are totally useless. The gods can scarcely save anyone else from the effects of the law of Karma since they are incapable of saving themselves. The principal aim of the writers of the Upanishads was, like that of Voltaire, to "crush the infamous thing" [institutional religion]; not only did the writers of the Upanishads succeed in this; they went beyond it. Certainly, many Indians failed to perceive the logical consequences of the law of Karma, and hence continued to frequent their temples; but the contradiction remained for all of that.

Finally, one's Karma, as I have already noted, is never destroyed or cancelled. Whatever one may do, the law must come into play and each one must return to the earth to receive his reward or to undergo his punishment. Thus, although reincarnation was at first conceived in the hope of attaining a survival after death, it eventually ended up as a ghastly trap: man, caught up in the machinery of the wheel of fortune, can never escape in any way whatever.

The Upanishads, however, having undermined the spiritual authority of the Brahmins, still envisaged one possible exit from the law of Karma's closed circle: Gnosticism. The man who, by means of Yoga, comes to experience the divinity of Self, glimpses the possibility of escape from the endless cycle of births by means of this new *knowledge*; the soul, liberated by its knowledge from its own subtle body containing the seeds of future reincarnations, can enter into nirvana, that is to say, can melt into the All, or universal Self, and having become itself impersonal, is liberated from its destiny.

Thus salvation is accorded to man by means of the magical power of Yoga—and by the suppression of religion properly speaking. To obtain this salvation, man has no further need of prayers; he has no further need of morality either: he has need only of knowledge, the knowledge gained by his experience of the fact of the identity of the Self and God. He who fails to attain to this knowledge, this gnostic realization of his true identity, must go on with his endless round of useless suffering, of reincarnations down through the millenia in this world.

I am well aware, of course, that some of our modern Gnostics have attempted to modify this picture somewhat. They have imagined in the vision of universal progress, for example, an amelioration of the lot of the soul as it advances from planet to planet and galaxy to galaxy (modern Gnosticism does not fail to follow the progress of current scientific developments with the liveliest kind of interest); it is sometimes believed that this kind of progress will lead to a progressively more remarkable perfection. In reality, nothing is less assured as far as the rigid law of Karma is concerned. For there is nothing to prevent the soul from lapsing back into old mistakes or losing its way, and hence falling back to the bottom of the reincarnational ladder and being obliged to start all over again moving through the cycle of births.

I would certainly not have wanted to be an Indian at the moment when these consequences of the Upanishad revolution began to be manifest to the adepts of this way. Fortunately, new elements entered into the picture to break the iron yoke of Karma and offer some slightly less grim and horrible prospects to anxious souls concerned about their destiny.

The Bhakti Movement

The religious skepticism which came to prevail in the north of India, being such an intellectual thing, could not dominate Indian religion indefinitely. Although it made possible an attenuation of Brahmin domination, it could not stand by itself since it had nothing to nourish the human heart. From the south, therefore, there came a kind of "Counter-Reformation," arising out of the peoples who were closer to the original paganism and accustomed to the idea of personal deities.

It was thus from the south that the Bhakti movement came—a movement emphasizing *devotions*, whose adepts considered themselves *servants* and *friends* of their gods: Krishna, Siva, Parvati, and others. In such devotional milieus, both the rigorism of strict Brahminism and the typical gnostic-type speculations were avoided; beliefs such as that the gods could in some fashion succor the unfortunate and that graces from above could be of help to those being crushed under the yoke of Karma still prevailed.

In these regards, the Bhakti movement naturally inspires sympathy, in spite of its tendency to dissolve into superstitions and even at times to slide into an unedifying eroticism. However that may be, the doctrine of reincarnation here becomes understood in a way that is more compatible with Christian concepts, that is to say, reincarnation is wholly subordinate to the will of God Who loves those whom He loves, Who comforts and guides them, and Who finally delivers them entirely from the cycle of births by placing them on the road of the Divine Way.

It was under the influence of this kind of thinking that Ramanuja, a Hindu theologian of the twelfth century A.D., wrote that God "could overcome the power of the law of Karma, in order to draw repentant sinners to Himself." Here we encounter a remarkable instance of Indian religious thought approaching the concepts of Judaism and Christianity. However, once this kind of question has been raised in Hinduism, what is to prevent the raising of much more fundamental questions? For instance: "If God can pardon, if God can by His grace save the afflicted sinner, why does He allow men to go on groaning under the law of Karma at all?"[19]

Footnotes

14. In other words, God (Brahman), according to this conception, is Himself the Self and the soul of each being.
15. It is believed that the first authors of the Upanishads were elderly priests who had left a regular religious life with its ritual obligations to "return to nature," no longer sacrificing on the altars but rather "within themselves." Thirsting for immortality, they came to despise the rites and doctrines they had formerly shared with other Brahmins. There could also have been, in these first esoteric groups, numbers of members of the Kshatriya, or warrior noble caste, who had decided to take up philosophy.
16. Here we encounter the old Divine Way of Vedic retribution.
17. That is to say, their soul has become perfect, and *perfectly itself*, by virtue of having gained the knowledge of its true (divine) identity.

18. This does not mean that Gnostics, on principle and without any reason, reject all the rules of individual and social morality; rather it means that, considering themselves identical to God, they are above all laws, whether human or divine. This is why, in apostolic times, the Gnostics were bitter enemies of Yahweh, the God of the Old Testament, Who was conceived by the Jews primarily as the Author of the *Law*. It was against such Gnostics that St. Paul and St. John affirmed so strongly the true "liberty of the children of God," which involves not the rejection but rather the assimilation of the law, become by the renewal of the Christian's heart like a spontaneous "instinct" or second nature—for those, that is, who have been baptized and animated by the Spirit of God (Rm 8:14).

19. Read Text VII in the Appendix.

PART TWO

THE CHRISTIAN DOCTRINE

OF THE

RESURRECTION

I

THE GOD OF THE CHRISTIANS

Summary. The God of the Christians: a personal God; a Creator God; a God responsible for physical evil; a God Who is the Author of grace.

A Personal God

I do not believe it is necessary to go into certain modern versions of the doctrine of reincarnation. What has been said about this doctrine up to this point really covers all the essential ground, for none of the modern theories provides any new departures or possibilities as far as the compatibility of reincarnation with Christianity is concerned. This is true regardless of one's particular reasons for subscribing to a belief in reincarnation: psychological reasons (dreams, hypnosis, experience of the beyond, etc.); or metaphysical reasons (an explanation for the inequality of the human condition, the necessity of justifying the existence of evil in this world and the ways of God to man). Regardless of how one handles these particular questions, the fact of the matter remains that the Christian view of the world is simply *different* from everything that we have considered up to now concerning reincarnation. It is now incumbent upon us to show what this "Christian difference" consists of.

Let us not make any mistake about this last remark. No one is constrained to be a Christian; but if he is one, he certainly has the right to an authentic Christianity, and for that, it is necessary to know what an authentic Christianity is. There is not any question here of a "freedom of conscience" about what one chooses to believe; the only question here is the question of the truth of the facts. Each one of us is *free* to opt either for a belief in the doctrine of reincarnation, or for a belief in the resurrection of the body; but it would simply be dishonest to claim to be able to believe in both, or, more especially, to imagine ourselves free to try to persuade others to adopt such a contradiction. We are no more able to do that than we are able to square the circle.

I would not dwell on this point quite so much if I had not actually heard the leaders of certain gnostic-style movements in Montreal trying to maintain that there was no incompatibility between Christianity and their systems which consider a belief in reincarnation legitimate.

"How will Christians react," I have asked such sectarian leaders, "when they realize that they cannot advance to the higher ranks or degrees in your scheme of things unless they adopt your belief in reincarnation?" And this is the kind of response I have received: "Once they arrive at that realization, they *see* [i.e., they will have acquired the proper *gnosis* and will then *know*] that reincarnation is a fact." But this does not resolve the contradiction; once reincarnation is considered to be a fact, authentic Christianity has disappeared. In other words, once they have arrived at this realization they will have ceased to be Christians!

To understand this we have to study the doctrine of reincarnation in the light of the Judeo-Christian revelation. I believe it is indispensable to begin this study by examining the Christian conception of God, for this conception is truly and obviously the keystone of the entire Christian edifice.

Blaise Pascal, in the celebrated *Memorial* of his conversion which was found sewn into his coat after his death, spoke of the

> . . . God of Abraham, God of Isaac, God of Jacob: not the god of the philosophers and savants . . . God of Jesus Christ. . . .

All of this does not constitute merely a literary expression or manner of speaking, or some kind of a sentimental assertion; it truly expresses a conception of God that goes right to the heart of what concerns us in this book.

It is only necessary to consult the article on God in any encyclopedia or philosophical dictionary in order to appreciate the profound truth of Pascal's simple declaration. The God fashioned by men down through the ages, by means of their subtle reasonings or intuitions, is almost always an abstract, theoretical God, a "God-idea," a God Who is "pure act," absorbed in His immobility and the contemplation of His own perfection to such an extent that He neither takes any interest in human beings nor answers their prayers. Or else this "God of the philosophers and savants" is an impersonal being, inextricably tied up with the world, some kind of a vague "cosmic energy" diffused through being or concentrated at some mysterious point that contains His essence; a God still "becoming," like the world itself. About this God it is often solemnly asserted that He has a "future"—a future that man, of course, deigns to accord to Him!

The conception of God found in the Bible is flatly opposed to this sort of abstract philosophical verbiage. The God of Abraham, Isaac and Jacob is a personal God, close to men; He has actually spoken to men in various ways and intervenes in human history. He is the God Who manifested Himself to men in Jesus Christ. For the Christian, Jesus is not merely a myth; nor is he merely a great prophet or seer, a holy man, or a religious genius; for the Christian, Jesus is *God made man*, and, as such, He is what Pascal, again, called

> . . . the true God of men . . . (Pascal, *Pensées*, Brunschvicq Edition, Fragment 547).

This Christian God is such that, in no way could I ever identify Him with my own *self*, even though He is closer to me, across both time and space, than I am to myself.

When we understand God's true nature, we understand why the Fathers of the Church were so insistent upon distinguishing Jesus of Nazareth from the various contemporaneous mythical and gnostic "gods" they knew about who were understood as being "cosmic energy;" for it was not in such "gods" as these that men would truly realize and fulfill themselves; rather, they would be dissolved and lose themselves.

But the personal "God of Jesus Christ, Who created man, body and soul, "in His image," decreed a destiny for man that entails not reincarnation, but resurrection.

A Creator God

This personal God is the Creator of the world as well as of each individual human soul.

But we must realize that the full meaning of this concept of *creation* was not immediately realized by the first Christian thinkers—nor, indeed, is it always completely understood by some Christians today.

Many people still imagine that, in the beginning, there already existed a body of unformed matter, a preexisting "chaos," which God, employing his cosmic power, "organized" into the world as we know it. Such an idea of God's role in creation is insufficient. Instead, we must take literally what is said in the prologue of the Gospel according to St. John:

> Through Him all things came to be; not one thing had its being but through Him (Jn 1:3).

The implications of this have not always been clearly seen. St. Justin, for instance, makes two different assertions about creation that cannot be reconciled. In a text implying that there was a preexistent matter, he says:

> We learned that, in the beginning, God, being all-good, created the world out of unformed matter, for the sake of man.

On the other hand, the same St. Justin declares the following about souls:

> We believe that, in the beginning, He made them, they *who did not exist before*, but who today, in choosing to please Him, will merit immortality (St. Justin, *First Apology*, 10:2-3).

This second text, with its mention of those "who did not exist before," implies the true idea of creation out of nothing and of passage from nonbeing to being.

Along these same lines, it is worth quoting a modern Catholic writer who declares that it would be idolatry to admit

> . . . the possibility of existence or of lives apart from the unique existence and life of God. Since God is unique, so is the existence of everything else, whether living or inanimate; each thing is equally unique, since, without exception, it shares in the unique existence of God (Fr. H. Lassait, *L'Actualité de la Catéchèse Apostolique*, Editions Présence, 1978).

What is idolatrous, or, more specifically, what is gnostic, is to deny that God can cause to exist outside of Himself separate and distinct beings who are also free and autonomous. Such a denial implies the substitution for the idea of *creation* the very different idea of *emanation*, which assumes that everything is necessarily part and parcel of God and is *not* created separate and distinct, free and autonomous.

And this latter idea, that nothing is distinct or separate from God, is, of course, the fundamental idea of the Upanishads, as it is of the Gnostics of every age; it implies the identification of the Self or "I" and God, of the Atman with the Brahman.[20]

For Christianity, as for Judaism, the very paradox and mystery of creation is that a personal and transcendent God has indeed created a world apart from Himself (though He remains no less totally responsible for creating and maintaining it in being). This is what the Creed *means* when it speaks of "God the Father Almighty, Creator of heaven and earth—" who rules His creation, as St. Irenaeus remarked, by the *hands* of His Word and His Spirit.

It is an understanding of this that cures us of the idealistic thinker's temptation to dismiss the reality of the world perceived by the senses and even of the possibility of personal survival after death as deluded and unsound; and that also cures us of the materialist's temptation to imagine God as merely "cosmic energy" or some kind of "world soul."

God really exists, and so do both the material and spiritual worlds. However, God exists by and in Himself with a *pure existence*, while the world participates in His existence and derives its being from Him at every instant.[21]

But even when we have said that, we have still not said everything. Many people, when they try to think about creation, tend to focus on the initial *moment* of creation, "in the beginning."[22] In this they are the disciples of the philosopher Descartes, who also conceived of creation in precisely this way. Thus Blaise Pascal aptly remarked about the philosophy of Descartes:

> I cannot really pardon Descartes: he wanted to formulate his entire philosophy without reference to God. Although he could not avoid giving God a role in starting up the world, he ignored God completely from then on (Pascal, *Pensées*, Brunschvicq Edition, Fragment 77).

However, the fact of the matter is just the opposite of what Descartes thought. The Christian conception of creation is not conceived most clearly by reflecting upon God's creation "in the beginning," but rather by reflecting upon the fact that nobody in the world around us has within himself the *reasons* for his own existence; it is in order to escape from the total *absurdity* of beings existing without any reason that we come to postulate God.

Let us consider, for example, my hand. How is it that my hand can exist from one second to the next, as I sit looking at it? Do I cause it to exist? If so, I also ought to possess the power either to will its continued existence or to deprive it of existence altogether at will. Was it enough that my parents simply procreated me in order that I should exist today and my hand along with me? No: I am quite conscious of the fact that my parents are powerless to will my continued existence or prevent my extinction. Therefore, my parents are not the ultimate *cause* of me.

Leaving aside my hand, I look at the world, the stars, the galaxies: how can all these things exist, right now, under my very eyes? For none of these things is *necessary*; none of them has to exist; none has within itself the reason for its own being. Any of these things can simply disappear without offending any principle of reason; indeed, what offends my reason—what staggers and overwhelms my mind, in fact—is the idea that all these things could simply be there without any cause for their existence, without any guarantee that they will go on existing from this moment.

If I go to the circus and watch a magician pull rabbits, ribbons, fish bowls filled with fish, or what have you, out of a hat, I am not surprised to hear children laughing almost hysterically at the spectacle. The magician shows them his empty hat; he shows them his empty hands and sleeves as well—yet he still manages to produce a profusion of very real things out of all this emptiness! Such is the situation of man faced with the existing universe. Intellectually speaking, there are only two possible solutions that offer themselves to his mind: 1) either everything that he sees is inexplicable and absurd (and, if so, what is the point of going on?); or else 2) there is a divine Magician somewhere able to pull out of His hat all the existing things that, as far as I can see, don't come from anywhere and are simply conjured up at this Magician's pleasure. It is this second image of a divine Magician that gives us the truest idea of the Christian conception of creation.

The metaphysicians of India, like Plato, came close to grasping the basic intuition about the nature of creation; but, in the end, they failed to grasp it because they could not conceive of God creating the world out of *nothing*, conjuring up something out of nowhere; they could not imagine God causing anything to exist *outside Himself*—beings who were both real and free, and yet wholly dependent upon Him and deriving everything from Him in Whom they "live, and move, and exist" (Ac 17:28).

In the later Upanishads, however—and, in particular, in the work of the great Hindu theologian Shankara (flourished A.D. 800)—the conception that is found is that the external created world is simply an illusion; our bodies, the dreams that haunt our sleep, even reincarnation itself are all nothing else but illusions and appearances, "such stuff as dreams are made on," as Shakespeare remarked. Only one being exists, God, identical to the Self in each of us; the Self is God, and God is the Self—thus do the Upanishads and Shankara teach, and outside of this closed circle, there is nothing.

St. Justin, in *Dialogue with Trypho*, is probably the first Christian thinker to pose clearly the question about creation, and to see the question in its proper light. Speaking with a mysterious "old man," he learns from the latter that Platonic philosophy tends to *veil*, rather than to *reveal*, the true face of God:

> "What, then, is philosophy?" the old man asked, "and what happiness does it bring?"
>
> I replied: "Philosophy is the science of being and the knowledge of truth. And happiness is the reward one gains from the knowledge and wisdom which philosophy procures."
>
> "But what is *Being*?" he asked.
>
> "That which is always the same, and always acts in the same way as the cause of everything that is, God . . . Everything that exists outside of God, and everything that will ever be apart from Him is corruptible, and can disappear, and thus no longer *be*. Only God is unengendered and incorruptible—these are precisely the characteristics that make him God—while everything else whatever, is engendered and corruptible" (St. Justin, *Dialogue with Trypho*, Chapter 5).

In the universe as seen by the Christian, there is no possibility of God not being present to every single one of His creatures, say, because certain ones of them are thought to be incapable of knowing Him, or because they refuse to keep Him in their minds. God always remains present and available to them notwithstanding; not only does He see each creature at every instant; He explicitly wills that each should continue to be and to be maintained in existence. And He acts to that same end.

For those who might assert that this would be impossible for God, let us think of a Johann Sebastian Bach improvising a fugue on the organ. A multitude of notes succeed one another at different pitches and rhythms; yet Bach is "present" to each note. If he sustains a note at one point, fingering arpeggios at another, he does not do so by accident or at random. The work proceeds in line with his knowledge of the pattern and plan of the music he wants to create and in accordance with his will to create that particular piece of music. We need to look at God somewhat in the same fashion, and remember that every note, even every dissonance, in the great hymn of the universe is the work of an artist who is aware of and concerned with even the tiniest details of his work.

A God Responsible for Physical Evil

We must understand—and we will devote an entire chapter to this topic—that God is not justified merely by supposing that He is unaware of evil, or that He is not concerned about it, or that He is powerless to remedy it. Nor is the problem solved by making man himself responsible for the evil that befalls him—owing to his actions in a previous existence. God was at work in those supposed previous existences every bit as much as He is at work now; hence the doctrine of reincarnation does not really explain the present sufferings of children, the gross inequalities of social conditions, or racial or sex discrimination.

A God Who Is the Author of Grace

Another conclusion that is even more decisive results from a careful study of the Christian revelation; this will show that the idea of reincarnation is simply incompatible with Christianity. It comes down to this: God, Who created man as we know him, that is, composed of both body and soul, nevertheless, as we also know from revelation, calls man to a beatitude which proceeds far beyond the possibilities and limits of this life. What God holds in reserve for man is not merely the happiness resulting from the perfect realization of his natural potentialities; it is rather an entering into a communion with God Himself, a participation in the happiness proper to God, a happiness which transcends all man's natural capacities.

It is remarkable that Christian theology of grace, that is, of *re*-creation or rebirth, first came into existence as a result of the Church's clashes with Gnosticism.[23] For the Gnostics, believing as they did that their "I" or Self was divine, it was only necessary to acquire a knowledge (*gnosis*) of this truth in order to be sure of being saved thereby. To this gnostic doctrine, the early Christians countered with St. John's teaching in the Prologue of his Gospel:

> But to all who did accept *Him*, He gave *power* to become children of God (Jn 1:11-12).

If this power is *given* by God, it therefore doesn't belong originally to man; man receives it, not by the practice of a special asceticism, nor by a particular kind of introspection nor ("transcendental") meditation, but rather by a conscious and willing faith in the "name" of Jesus.

Moreover, this particular Christian doctrine speaks decisively against the notion of reincarnation. If the call of man to a special type of communion with God stems from a *power* acquired by faith, what is the point of the thousands of incarnations through which man would hope to arrive at the perfection of his being? Even if he were to succeed in this manner to eliminate all his faults and to do all the good within his power, the fact would remain that he was still as far as ever from the higher state of a divine communion to which he is being called by God and of which St. Paul says that

> ... We teach what Scripture calls the things that no eye has seen and no ear has heard, things beyond the mind of man, all that God has prepared for those who love Him (1 Cor 2:9).

What God has promised is above and beyond the natural aspirations of our hearts and souls. This is why Judaism, which expected perfect justification before God to come from obeying the Law, was seen to be insufficient by the disciples of Jesus, who assigned the final beatitude of man, not merely to the sum total of his good works, but rather to a divine gift of love that went beyond all justice and merit:

> Think of the love that the Father has lavished on us, by letting us be called God's children; and that is what we are ...
> My dear people, we are already the children of God but what

we are to be in the future has not yet been revealed; all we know is, that when it is revealed, we shall be like Him because we shall see Him as He really is (1 Jn 3:1-2).

The Christian certainly is strictly obliged to carry out good works; but these good works are above all the *response* of his love to a divine love given first to him, inviting him to a final and absolute communion in this same divine love.

Let us try to explain further this distinction—very important to our overall topic—by the following comparison. Let us suppose that a father promises to buy his son a sports car if he does well on his examinations at school. Let us then suppose further that the son does do well on his school examinations. Can we thereby assert that the son has somehow *earned* or *merited* the sports car in strict justice? It is not the son's success on his examinations which binds and obliges the father to buy the car; rather, it is the father's *promise*, that was freely (and gratuitously) given to his son in the matter. And so it is for the beatitude offered to the Christian by a God Who is bound to accord him that beatitude not because it has been merited by good works but precisely because it was promised.

Some Gospel Examples

Let us also examine the Gospels on this matter. A parable illustrates what I am trying to demonstrate here; and even though it is not directly related to reincarnation, it can quite appropriately be applied to that subject.

A landowner hired workers for his vineyard; he made an agreement to pay those who started the first thing in the morning one denarius for the whole day's work. During the course of the day he hired other workers, promising to pay a "fair wage." At the end of the day, bringing together all the workers hired, he paid each one a denarius without distinction. The workers hired first then complained against the landowner:

> "The men who came last," they said, "have done only one hour, and you have treated them the same as us, though we have done a heavy day's work in all the heat" (Mt 20:12).

The landowner then replied to one of them:

"My friend, I am not being unjust to you; did we not agree on one denarius? Take your earnings and go. I choose to pay the last comer as much as I pay you. Have I no right to do what I like with my own? Why be *envious* because I am *generous?*" (Mt 20:13-15).

This parable certainly has primary reference to the case of pagans being admitted to the Kingdom, like the workers of "the eleventh hour," on the same basis as the Chosen People, who had labored long for the advent of that Kingdom. However, the lesson of the parable also has a bearing on the doctrine of reincarnation; for what purpose is served by a thousand reincarnations if God can grant eternal beatitude according to His own good pleasure at the end of a single life?

Another illustration of the same kind is provided by St. Luke. Jesus, on the cross, was bitterly reproached by one of the two criminals being crucified along with Him. The other thief then spoke up and rebuked the first one:

"Have you no fear of God at all?" he said. "You got the same sentence as He did, but in our case we deserved it; we are paying for what we did. But this man has done nothing wrong. Jesus," he said, "remember me when you come into your kingdom."

"Indeed, I promise you," He replied, "today you will be with me in paradise" (Lk 23:40-43).

We see here clearly how the law of Karma is incompatible with the law of love instituted by Christ from the height of the cross. The law of Karma demands rigorous, inexorable justice; the law of the cross is all pardon and gratuitous gift.

Perhaps I might recall in this connection how the Old Testament prepared the way for the vision realized in the New Testament. The call to the great elect of God portrayed in the Old Testament is never foreseeable and does not depend in any way upon the merit of the one elected, but simply upon the mercy of the One Who elects—Who is reported in Scripture as saying: "I have compassion on whom I will, and I show pity to whom I please" (Ex 33:19; Rm 9:15).

The Psalmist expresses the same point with a slight touch of humor when he tells the "just man:"

> In vain you get up earlier,
> And put off going to bed,
> Sweating to make a living,
> Since He provides for His
> Beloved as they sleep" (Ps 127:2).

In concluding this chapter, let us take note of the fact that Gnosticism itself arrived by an unexpected path at the conclusion which renders reincarnation perfectly superfluous.

This is so because Gnosticism too found no efficacy for salvation in good works and, indeed, preached, if not "salvation by faith alone," certainly "a salvation assured solely by a *knowledge* of one's own divinity." Gnostic-style knowledge was understood as a sort of "grace" or "gift of light:" a discovery of the true human condition, a "revelation" of the identity of the Self and of God which by itself was supposed to liberate the members of the elect from the anguish of future reincarnations.

Thus we Christians have two very strong reasons for not believing in reincarnation, two reasons that demonstrate the futility of the reincarnational idea. For God, Who created us and maintains us in being, has called us to a beatitude with Him that far exceeds all possible aspirations; furthermore, we do not of ourselves possess the *power* to save ourselves, even through a thousand reincarnations; salvation is given from above. Since that is the case, what would be the point of any reincarnations at all?

Even so, the picture is still not complete. We shall see the further uselessness and futility of the idea of reincarnation when we consider the relationship between God and man the sinner.[24]

Footnotes

20. In the more refined Gnosticisms, the identification of the Self and God is spoken of (rather than identification of the "I" and God) precisely in order to indicate that the individual "I" is nothing else but an appearance and a portion of universal being, without any specific personality. Let us note in passing the incoherence of certain Christians who claim to experience no difficulty in admitting the Indian conception of God according to which He is in everything and everything is in Him, or in imagining in consequence that their own self is identical to God. St. Justin long ago anticipated the response to such imagining when he asked what "generosity" God could have shown in saving what is personal to Him anyway [namely, man], "for in that case He would only be saving Himself!" (St. Justin, Fragment 8). When a Christian reaches the point where he has no difficulty in admitting that which denies the very principle of redemption in and through Jesus Christ, it means he has already strayed far from Christianity.

21. Let us note what Fr. A.D. Sertillanges says so admirably about this in his book *L'Idee de Creation et ses Retentissements en Philosophie* (Paris, 1945, p. 68): "The idea that created beings tend towards nothingness, taken by itself, does not express anything very significant, for nothingness amounts to, precisely, nothing, and hence cannot really be the object of any tendency. That which *it* tends rather toward being; not only does it tend towards being, it tends toward the perfection of its being. This is so because it participates in the being of God to Whom belongs the fullness of all being. Thus, what participates in Him can have no other law than that of more perfect participation, that is, the perfection of one's being. To realize God's intention in creating us must be our chief intention."

22. In fact, the very idea of a *moment* of creation is an illusion since prior to creation itself, there were not any moments or motion at all; there was not yet any *before* or *after*, and consequently, there was not yet any time.

23. This can be very clearly seen in St. Irenaeus in particular; he derives from 1 Th 5:23 his conception of a *tripartite* composition of man who, by nature, is not merely composed of body and soul, but, by baptism, becomes composed of body, soul, and *spirit*, spirit consisting for him of the divine grace infused by God to raise us to a higher destiny. "That we originate as a body, taken from the earth, and a soul which receives God's Spirit, no one will deny" (St. Irenaeus, *Exposition and Refutation of Gnosticism*, III.22.2). This conception amounts to a very early formulation of what the Council of Trent, speaking of the "justice" that interiorly sanctifies baptized persons, calls "a divine gift that renews us in the most intimate part of the soul" (Session VI, Chapter 7). We may also recall Canons 10 and 11 of the same Council; what came to be called "sanctifying grace" had thus already been indicated by St. Irenaeus.

24. Read Text VIII in the Appendix.

II

GOD AND PHYSICAL EVIL

Summary. Attempts to justify God's ways to man; reincarnation; other solutions. Examination of the solutions: absolute evil; Maya; Karma. The Bible and the evil of the world.

We have now seen how the problem of evil affected belief in the doctrine of reincarnation.

On the one hand, it was believed that this doctrine *justified* God with regard to the presence of evil in the human condition—pain, sickness, social inequalities, etc.; on the other hand, the connection between the doctrine of reincarnation and the idea of *retribution* posed the problem of human *sin* (although not in a completely clear and precise manner).

Now we must examine in greater detail how Christianity proposes solutions to these same two problems: the existence of evil in the world and the existence of sin in man. The Christian solutions differ markedly from the Indian solutions.

Reincarnation as a Theodicy

In Part One, I described how Aryan domination was established in the north of India. Around 1500 B.C., light-skinned tribes, related to those inhabiting Asia Minor, descended into the Indian subcontinent via Iran and the Punjab and settled in Northwest India; from there they swarmed into the valley of the Ganges.

We gather from reading the early Vedic hymns that this Aryan invasion, like all invasions, was a painful and harrowing experience. The light-skinned conquerors despised the dark-skinned indigenous populations whom they literally regarded as incarnate demons; they called them unflattering names and reduced them to the lowest rank on the social scale, designating them as Sudras.

However, it appears that it was out of this same misery and suffering that India drew the inspiration for profound reflections on the problem of evil. Like other pagan peoples, the Aryans presented their god Indra as an omniscient, all-powerful, perfect being. When the moment came to explain to the subdued, subject classes how it came about that this omniscient, all-powerful and perfect god allowed some human beings to be born in the highest, privileged castes, while others were born to the outcasts, Aryan metaphysics was put to a difficult test.

The reaction of the Brahmin theologians to whom the task of explanation fell was, quite understandably, to try to justify Indra by developing a *theodicy*. This word "theodicy," which we owe to the German philosopher Leibnitz, means any systematic effort to *justify* God for His ways to man and to explain how He can allow evil to exist in the world. The word comes from the Greek words, *Dikê*, "justice," and *Theou*, "of God."

A theodicy is only possible in those religions which both teach a lofty conception of God's perfection and make God responsible for the operation of the world. Such was the Vedic religion of the Aryans. How could Indra's honor be salvaged in the light of the gross social inequalities that were the results of the Aryan invasions? Eventually the principal theodicy that was developed accomplished this by making use of a religious belief already accepted by the indigenous inferior classes: reincarnation. It was explained that inferior social status was due neither to Indra nor to Aryan domination, but rather to the individual malice of those who suffered, to faults committed by them in a previous existence. Why was a Sudra born of seed deposited in the womb of an outcast woman rather than in that of a woman of the Kshatriya or Brahmin castes? It was for the Sudra to examine his previous existences to discover the reason . . . I am, of course, being deliberately ironic here, as I am also simplifying things somewhat; however, the essence of what I am saying *was* present in the Indian idea of reincarnation as it was found in history.

Let us examine more seriously how the doctrine fares as a solution to the problem of evil when compared with some other solutions that have been proposed.

Other Solutions to the Problem of Evil

Generally speaking, in philosophical discussions of the problem of evil in the world a distinction is often made between *physical evil* and *moral evil*. Physical evil is external and impersonal. Moral evil, however, consists principally in free and deliberate acts against God, God's laws, and humanity itself.

Let us remember as we attempt to discuss these things that the existence of evil in the world is in no way caused by religion or philosophy; the evil is there; it affects believers and unbelievers alike. Religion and philosophy merely attempt to explain this evil. Too often this point is forgotten in discussions of the matter. Also, among the explanations provided by religion or philosophy, some are more satisfying than others.[25]

For the sake of simplicity, I will cite five distinct schools of thought in the matter of explaining the existence of evil in the following paragraphs.

1. *The Aesthetic School:* On the whole, the world is considered good and beautiful. That which we perceive as evil or ugly is nothing but a dissonance useful in insuring the overall harmony of the whole. The evils with which the world is afflicted can serve to prevent even greater evils: if the water of the oceans were ice, there would certainly no longer be shipwrecks, but, on the other hand, there wouldn't be much chance of navigation either; nor could human beings derive so much of their substance from the reservoir of animal and vegetable life that constitutes the oceans.

2. *The Moralizing School:* The evils with which the world is afflicted, volcanoes, earthquakes, etc., serve to help form human character. Those who never suffer or know adversity know noth

ing. A world without suffering would be a world of egoists and of the insufferably proud.

3. *The Freedom-Loving School:* Freedom is the greatest of goods, but the majority of evils, such as illnesses, are the consequences of the deficient use which men make of their liberty; we need think only of abuses of the environment, sexual excesses, etc. God does not intervene to stop these abuses because He respects human freedom and wants to give men the opportunity to learn from experience the evil consequences of their actions for themselves and others in order that they may learn responsible freedom.

4. *The Idealistic School:* The evil that we perceive with our senses is nothing but an illusion belonging to this physical world which is itself an illusion. He who turns away from this illusion moves towards truth, towards ultimate Reality, and is no longer concerned with the evil of this world. He who discovers the identity of the Self and God no longer experiences evil (as in Buddhism and various Gnosticisms).

5. *The Realistic School:* Once God has decided to create the world, He accepts the evil that would necessarily be inherent in any finite creation; everything that is created is dependent and limited. It is this contingency and limitation of being that causes its imperfection, and the evils we experience stem from the imperfection of the beings that surround us.

It is obvious that each of these schools of thought possesses some insight into the problem of evil, although it is equally obvious that some schools of thought merit greater attention from us than others.

Examination of Some of the Solutions

A. *Absolute Evil.* Certain Gnosticisms (for example, the Iranian one) have pictured the history of the world as an equal conflict between two absolute forces: the force of Good and the force of Evil. The chief difficulty in this concept resides in the fact that the very notion of an "absolute" evil is inconceivable. In order to act as a "force," evil must first exist; but, to exist is already a *good.* Moreover, an absolute good existing in the face of an absolute evil would not be possible because such a good would be *limited* by the existence of the evil; neither principle, in fact, could be absolute confronted with the other.

B. *Maya.* The type of Gnosticism developed by the Hindu theologian Shankara was not wrong within its own terms of reference to develop an *idealistic* solution to the problem of evil. According to the solution, everything outside of the Self, including the soul's subtle body as well as the body itself, the external world, the world of dreams, and, finally, reincarnation itself, is nothing but *maya*, or illusion. Hence evil, which belongs to this illusory world outside the self, is only an *appearance*.

Let us be very careful to take note of the fact that the advancing of such a system by Shankara and other Hindu theologians in no way represents merely a manner of speaking. When Jesus demands of His disciples that they should "hate" their fathers, mothers, brothers and sisters (Lk 14:26), this, of course, *is* a manner of speaking, as is the following well-known private revelation of God to St. Catherine of Siena:

> Do you know who you are and Who I am? If you know the answers to both questions, you will be happy: for I am He Who *is*, while *you are she who is not!* (Bl. Raymond of Capua, *The Life of St. Catherine of Siena*, Chapter 10).

It is manifest that, if St. Catherine of Siena had *truly* not existed, God could not have entered into any kind of dialogue with her. . . .

But Shankara and his disciples were not speaking figuratively; they wanted to be taken literally. They held that the self was quite literally divine, and that apparent sufferings, the bad fruits of sins committed in a previous existence, simply did not ultimately exist. If pressed about how human beings were nevertheless affected, indeed often crushed, by the appearance or *illusion* they had of suffering, these Hindu theologians were apparently unable to produce a serious or satisfying explanation.

We Christians, of course, believe that the evils that afflict us are real: Jesus did not merely appear to die on the cross. St. Paul may speak of how light our tribulations are when compared with the "weight of eternal glory" (2 Cor 4:18) to come in heaven; he does not, for all of that, cease to believe that we must in a very real way "share Christ's sufferings so as to share in His glory" (Rm 8:17). To provide a solution to the problem of evil and suffering simply by denying the existence of evil and suffering is hardly satisfactory. What is the use of a philosophy that is merely repeated in the classroom but has no application to the life we actually live? If the external world is nothing but an appearance, why do idealistic philosophers bother to go to the doctor when they are sick or hurry to catch their buses every morning? Shankara himself provides the example of a man who sees a rope, jumps, because he thinks it is a snake, discovers his illusion, and then proceeds on with no further fear of being bitten. . . .

C. *Karma*. I have already described the attempt of the system built on the doctrine of reincarnation to justify God's ways to man and the existence of evil in the world. I cited at that point (Chapter IV of Part One) a Buddhist text to the effect that Brahma, "the lord of all the multitudes that have been born," was "unjust" and had decreed "the misfortune of the whole universe." Otherwise, this Buddhist text asked pertinently, why would Brahma not intervene, since "the world is in such disorder?" (*Bhuridatta Jataka*, No. 543, v. 153c.).

Eventually, this line of thought almost inevitably imposes itself upon whoever attempts to maintain that God is both omnipotent and good.

Mainstream Hindu thought, however, wanted to exonerate God and make man alone responsible for the evils that weighed him down; these evils were interpreted as the deserved consequences of sins committed in a previous existence. It is worth noting that a not dissimilar conception was to be found even among the ancient Hebrews. Job's friends, for example, are eloquent proponents of a similar point of view; if Job is suffering misfortunes, it must be because of sins that he has committed, consciously or unconsciously, either during the course of his life, or, perhaps, while still in his mother's womb. It is therefore just that he should be punished and he has no one to blame but himself for what happens to him.

Job, of course, refuses to accept this explanation for his woes; eventually Yahweh Himself condemns the view of Job's friends and affirms instead that evil is a mystery which He, Yahweh, alone really understands. At this point, Job finally concedes:

> I know that you are all-powerful:
>   what you conceive, you can perform.
> I am the man who obscured your designs
>   with my empty-headed words.
> I have been holding forth on matters I cannot understand
>   on marvels beyond me and my knowledge (Jb 42:2-3).

One of the most implausible things about the theory of Karma is that it seeks a too-complicated explanation of the evils that afflict man. The simple plan of natural forces at work suffices to explain many of these evils. As Pascal says in one of his best known *Thoughts*:

> Man is nothing but a reed, the most fragile in nature . . .
> It is hardly necessary that the whole universe should take up arms against him; a single drop of water suffices to kill him (Pascal, *Pensées*, Brunschvicq Edition, Fragment 347).

However, let us not be too quick to dismiss the old philosophers who tried to look beyond the obvious causes of evil and who turned towards God Himself to demand an explanation for the evil in the world. There is more in this problem than a simple question of fact. For example, I have no trouble accepting the fact that carnivorous animals feed on herbivorous ones, or the fact that the lava flowing down the side of a volcano destroys all the vegetation in its path. However, I am already less willing to accept the destruction of my vineyards by that same lava. I am quite unwilling that a carnivorous animal should threaten me. Even when we might be willing to accept in theory that some evil may be inherent in the operation of the world, we are still unwilling to accept the evil that affects us; we instinctively revolt against it, and experience it as an injustice and as something that ought not to happen in the world *as it should be*.

Visiting a prison, it is possible to encounter prisoners who have robbed, killed or raped innocent people, but who are nevertheless heard to complain that they are being treated *unjustly* by being incarcerated, that no one has the right to punish them thus. It is easy to sneer at this kind of behavior but it shows that in the human heart there is an almost overwhelming conviction that man was created for happiness and that he should not have to suffer unhappiness. A *Thought* of Pascal, again, comes to mind in this connection:

> What is natural for animals, we call misery in man; by this we see that since man's nature resembles that of the animals, it must be a nature fallen from a higher state. For who is unhappy at not being king except a king who has been deposed? (Pascal, *Pensées*, Brunschvicq Edition, Fragment 409).

Even when a disobedient child is at fault for something he has done, he still expects his mother to get him out of the jam he has gotten himself into; in his humiliation, he will accept her correction and words which establish his guilt. There is one thing he will not accept, though, and that is being left by his mother to stew in his own juice. It is the same with man as far as the suffering which God permits is concerned; man will accept and suffer affliction; he will even invent theories about sins committed in an earlier existence to explain his sufferings. What he will never accept, however, is that a God Who is good could simply be *indifferent* to his afflictions and sufferings.

The Bible and the Evil of the World

The Bible as a whole went beyond Job's views and attempted to provide a precise explanation for the afflictions that we suffer. According to the Bible's account of Original Sin, Adam, the first man, was created for happiness; the material universe was placed under his sway and was to be for him a garden of delights. A companion, Eve, was created for him to take away the solitude of his heart. But this first human couple revolted against God; the eating of the "forbidden fruit" meant a violation of God's commandment and broke the original covenant God had made with Adam. As a result of Adam's rebellion against God, the material universe revolted against *him*, and henceforth produced thorns and brambles; the flesh revolted against the spirit; man even turned against his companion and subjected her to his caprices. Thus it was that the order and equilibrium of creation was upset, and evil entered everywhere—as the consequence of *sin*.

In this biblical explanation, as in the explanations provided in Indian religion, the divine transcendence is respected; an explanation of the existence of moral evil is provided, namely, that it is the consequence of man's sin and the punishment visited upon him for that sin. Beyond these similarities, however, there are two important differences between the Indian system and the biblical system.

First of all, in the Indian system the notion of sin is not brought to the fore. It appears that in the Indian context sin is not seen as first and foremost an offense against God that brings evil in its train. Evil is rather seen as a matter of *power*. In a closed universe there is supposed to reside a certain fixed amount of baleful and maleficent power; when there is more power here, there will be less elsewhere and so on. What is required of God in this situation—if, in fact, He truly does exist, and has sufficient knowledge and power—is that He act as a kind of referee to maintain some kind of equilibrium between the powers of good and evil and to prevent the latter from getting out of hand. Within this kind of framework the law of Karma functions with a kind of inescapable fatality. Whoever has accumulated in himself the seed of not living right will inevitably reap the fruit he has sown; whoever has accumulated the seed of living right will enjoy the good fruit of that. All this is required by the good order of things which functions for the benefit of power; whoever proves to have the most power is automatically found to be functioning within the order of things. Meanwhile, God is far above it all; God merely sees to it that the world continues to go on, and that no preponderance of *either good or evil* upsets the equilibrium of its operations.

The Bible, however, especially the New Testament, depicts God as being a great deal more concerned, not only about external evils but even about what man thinks. Man's sin offends and wounds God *personally*. If God is sometimes presented as a potentate touchy about His own honor, ready for revenge even down to the thousandth generation, the fact nevertheless remains that the waywardness of man tortures and torments Him as if man were His own son. God does not accept that man should bring about his own destruction, thus disfiguring also the image of God that man carries in his nature. God punishes man in order to correct him, in order to raise him up and restore him to his original perfection. In spite of the fact that this biblical explanation of the nature of evil is so different from that of the Indians, there is, nevertheless, some correspondence between it and the Indian conception of retribution. Where the gap between the two conceptions becomes unbridgeable, though, is at the point where the law of Karma is compared with the "law" of Christ's cross. Christianity delivers the last possible word about the consequences of sin: God Himself died in expiation of it! We will return to this point in the next chapter.

A further point to note about the differences between the Indian and the biblical explanations of evil, however, is that the Indian solution never amounts to anything but an intellectual, philosophical solution (except perhaps in the Bhakti movement). But the greatest weakness of any merely intellectual or philosophical solution to the problem of evil is that even if it commends itself to the reason, it doesn't succeed in touching the heart. The sick man listening to specialists discussing the nature of his case at the foot of his bed, gets small comfort or alleviation from it. For it really *is* small comfort merely to understand the reasons for one's suffering. The law of Karma may indeed explain social inequality or caste discrimination, but it is powerless to provide any remedy for them. In this respect, Christianity is seen to be plainly superior either to the closed circle of Hinduism, or even to a Judaism narrowly concentrated around a rigorist conception of Law. Christianity is not content merely to teach the truth that the evil of the world stems principally from man's sin;

Christianity goes on to affirm that God does not abandon the sinner to the consequences of his sin; indeed God seeks out the sinner as the shepherd seeks out his lost sheep. God always welcomes back the Prodigal Son after each of the latter's escapades. Thus it is that Christianity possesses a solution to the problem of evil every bit as rigorous and logical as the Indian conception—yet ultimately more complete and more satisfying.[26]

Footnotes

25. I follow very closely here the very interesting book of Wendy Doniger O'Flaherty, *The Origins of Evil in Hindu Mythology*, University of California Press, Berkeley, 1976.
26. Read Texts IX and X of the Appendix.

III

GOD AND THE SIN OF THE WORLD

Summary. Moral evil: sin. Expiatory suffering. The law of the cross.

I believe that it is worth recalling again, at the very beginning of this chapter, what I have already said before, namely, that the existence of evil in the world is anterior to the existence of all philosophies and all religions: they only attempt to explain the evil that is already there. I myself know certain Christians who, in their hearts, seem actually to resent Christ's death on the cross. They seem to imagine that, except for this death on the cross, life here below would be nothing but "love, delight and music." I am again reminded of a poem by the young Arthur Rimbaud, who so often functions in a kind of Greek chorus commenting on all our human temptations to revolt:

> I believe in Thee, Divine Mother,
> I believe!
> Aphrodite of the sea! Oh, the way is hard;
> That other God has bound us to his cross!
> Flesh, marble, flower, Venus—in Thee I believe . . . !
>
> The winds of love have passed us in the night.
> Yet in the sacred grove, that threatening shade,
> They stand in majesty, those forms:
> The Gods, whose eyes the ivy tries to hide—
> The Gods stand watching man and the unending World
> (Arthur Rimbaud, *Complete Works*, Translated from the French by Paul Schmidt, New York, Harper, 1975, pp. 21 and 24).

The truth is, though, that in this supposed pagan paradise in which Rimbaud believed to the exclusion of Christianity, if we view it as it actually existed before the coming of Christ—or in the many attempts that have been made to revive it since in the course of history—we will find the themes of egotism, misery, and injustice. In every generation martyrs have appeared who prefer to pass through the fire or be delivered to wild beasts rather than be a part of such a paganism as Rimbaud celebrates.

The greatest evils in the world are rather those that come from man himself, who, though he possesses intelligence, is able to make the world literally unlivable, both for himself and for others—not merely through ignorance, for ignorance does in a sense excuse, but purely and simply through evil will and uncontrolled passions. The evil that is in man is *sin*. Sin is not an abstraction, but rather a real expression in us of pride, cupidity, envy, jealousy, gluttony, or immoderate concupiscence, and so on; sin leads us to our own destruction and to the destruction of all who are around us or approach us.

Moral Evil: Sin

As I have indicated, the notion of sin underwent only a rudimentary development in ancient India. The proof of this is the persistent appearances of Gnosticism that situated evil not in the evil will of man but rather in his lack of *knowledge*. But who does not understand that the more intelligent and knowledgeable a criminal is, the more dangerous he is?

From the earliest times, human beings have believed that they could exonerate themselves from their faults and acts of violence by pretending that they had been victims of "evil spirits"—"the devil made them do it." These malign spirits supposedly took possession of men temporarily and forced them to commit acts which they afterwards regretted. Adam blamed the companion God had made for him for having given him the forbidden fruit; Eve blamed the serpent. When King Saul twice tried to pin David to the wall with his spear, the Bible charitably recounts that "an evil spirit" took possession of him and "he fell into a fit of frenzy while he was in his house" (1 S 18:10). In somewhat the same fashion, Indian religion saw in moral evil a kind of "force" or "power" distributed throughout the world and necessary for its proper functioning. Thus, in a sense, following their dharma, the thief was not really guilty of stealing nor the serpent of biting.

I do not wish to deny that, little by little, a true moral sense developed in India. I have already recalled the principal articles of what I called an Indian decalogue: nonviolence, truth, purity, good will, mercy, patience, and so on. We could only wish these things were more respected in the West! However, in the case of India, as in the case of Greece, these virtues developed out of social necessities and natural good sense rather than out of the tenets of the prevailing religion.

Nevertheless the moral code that did develop, did come to dominate the law of Karma: it was by practicing the virtues that one might expect a reward in the next world and a fortunate reincarnation back into this one. Conversely, it was by despising these virtues that one reaped punishment in the shadowy world to come and a miserable reincarnation back into this one. On this point, Indian religion did not differ that much, at least on the surface, from Judaism or even from Christianity. We have to look more deeply into the matter in order to see that there still remained a great difference, indeed an opposition, between the Christian and the Indian views.

The Indians would not have been able to recognize the necessity for reward and punishment for the actions of a previous existence if they had not recognized that these actions were either morally good or bad. However, the moral essence that they did assign to human actions, as I have been trying to explain, was not equivalent to what we in the West, with our Christian antecedents understand as authentically moral. The reason for this was that the Indians did not assign to the *will* the role we consider necessary in moral actions. The Indian moral code was primarily empirical; it arose from observation of the actual mores and behavior of the people living in communities. Moreover, once the code was established, failure to observe it was quite as serious whether one voluntarily transgressed it or accidentally transgressed it. If one touched someone "impure," one was automatically soiled, whether or not one had willed the action. From this it resulted quite naturally—at least as far as the educated class or the intellectuals were concerned—and they are always principally the ones who ask and answer questions such as these—that transgressions of the code became primarily questions of *ignorance*, rather than any wish or will to transgress it.

John Henry Cardinal Newman has given us an unforgettable description of a person who understands morality in this fashion:

> We find men possessed of many virtues, but proud, boastful, fastidious, and reserved. Why is this? It is because they think and act as if there were nothing objective in their religion; it is because conscience to them is not the word of a lawgiver, as it ought to be, but the dictate of their minds and nothing more; it is because they do not look through and beyond their own minds to their Maker, but are engrossed in notions of what is due to themselves, to their own dignity and their own consistency. Their conscience has become a mere self-respect. (John Henry Cardinal Newman, *The Idea of a University*, Edited with an Introduction and Notes by Martin J. Svaglic, New York, Holt, Rinehart and Winston, 1964, p. 146).

The Pharisees, at the time of Jesus, in an all-too-human way, contradicted the spirit of the religion they professed, and fell into the same way of thinking. The parable of the Pharisee and the tax collector condemns this way of thinking only too plainly:

> The tax collector stood some distance away, not daring even to raise his eyes to heaven; but he beat his breast and said, "God, be merciful to me a sinner." This man, I tell you, went home again at rights with God; the other did not (Lk 18:13-14).

The morality enjoined by Jesus is not what a man requires of himself according to his own measure or standard; it is what God requires of him according to a measure that God has established—indeed, this measure constitutes the fundamental principle of all religion, for the word religion means nothing else but the state of being *tied ("relié")* to God.

In the case of Christianity, therefore, the idea of retribution is not a matter of man measuring up to his own standards; it is a function of man's encounter with God. God, Who created man (and *re*-created him in the order of grace) requires a certain standard of behavior from him. When man willfully and deliberately refuses the obedience to God entailed in this relationship, he directly offends his Master and his Judge. The question of retribution is thus not a mere abstract or juridical question; it becomes personal. God may decide to pardon or not to pardon, but He will reward or punish according to His own standards. Man's destiny lies not merely in the accomplishment of a fatal law of nature; man's destiny is fulfilled as a consequence of the decisions of a divine will.

Fundamentally, this is the reason why reincarnation is irreconcilable with Christianity. For even if one conceded to man the power to be reincarnated down through millenia, in order to expiate faults committed in previous existences, the pardon for those faults, according to the authentic Christian view, would come neither from the multitude of punishments endured nor from their number or extent, but rather uniquely from the divine will which pardons or does not pardon, which cancels out an offense or decides to retain it.

I have already cited the example of the conversion *in extremis* of the Good Thief on the cross. Jesus did *not* say to him: "Your expiation has been sufficient; henceforth you shall be in the paradise you have earned." Jesus said: "Today you will be with me in Paradise" (Lk 23:14). Jesus spoke here in His own name, following His own *personal* decision. In the context of such divine mercy and grace, the idea of reincarnation loses its sense; it would only be intelligible as something imposed by God; however, that He has so imposed any such thing is nowhere contained in His revelation to mankind.[27]

Expiatory Suffering

But does this description of a "gratuitous" pardon from God

do justice to the full Christian position? If God *can* pardon, without any expiation on the part of the sinner, then, why does He permit, for example, the suffering of innocent children? Why, indeed, did the innocent Christ have to suffer and die, and why do we? Oscar Wilde, in his *De Profundis*—in which both the best and the worst are to be found—has touched upon this subject very pertinently:

> I remember talking once on this subject [of suffering] to one of the most beautiful personalities I have ever known; a woman whose sympathy and noble kindness to me, both before and since the tragedy of my imprisonment have been beyond power and description . . . I recall distinctly how I said to her that there was enough suffering in one narrow London lane to show that God did not love man, and that wherever there was any sorrow, though but that of a child in some little garden weeping over a fault that it had not committed, the whole face of creation was completely marred. I was entirely wrong. She told me so, but I could not believe her. I was not in the sphere in which such belief was to be attained. Now it seems to me that love of some kind is the only possible explanation of the extraordinary amount of suffering that there is in the world. I cannot conceive of any other explanation. I am convinced that there is no other, and that if the world has indeed, as I have said, been built of sorrow, it has been built by the hands of love, because in no other way could the soul of man, for whom the world was made, reach the full stature of its perfection. Pleasure for the beautiful body,[28] but pain for the beautiful soul (Oscar Wilde, *De Profundis*, in *The Portable Oscar Wilde*, New York, Viking, 1946, pp. 528-29).

Here we must realize that we are once again touching upon a question already raised, the question of the existence of physical evil. We have already observed on this subject that, in a world such as ours, it was inevitable that there would be suffering and even death—at least for the creatures below man. Certainly God could have created a world made out of inanimate rocks alone. There would have been no suffering in such a world, but there would not have been any plants either; nor any herbivorous animals, nor any carnivorous ones either. It is not clear that the world would have been any better for all that.

But the whole problem becomes more complicated with the appearance of man. The Book of Genesis informs us that man was originally set the task of cultivating the earth, a task that was not initially complicated by the growth of thorns and brambles; nor did man have to die originally. It was because of sin that man's miseries and sufferings entered the world. This explanation bears some resemblance to the one advanced by the proponents of reincarnation in that man's suffering *today* comes from an *antecedent fault* (that of Adam and his descendants). One may even in this fashion justify the suffering of children: they were not the ones who sinned; it was their parents, at any rate, their first parents. Though it is unacceptable to our modern sensibilities that anyone should suffer for the faults of another—children for the faults of their parents—we ourselves in the twentieth century go on multiplying the innocent victims of our wars, and it would never occur to us to blame the originators of these wars. But in the case of children's suffering, we presume to be able to demand an accounting from God Himself about it, almost as if the modern mind were disposed to accept the idea that such a demand implies, namely, that God might regularly intervene to prevent miraculously the effects of causes that we ourselves have set in motion, for example, those causing the sufferings of children. How many others, sons of the rationalism of Descartes, might see in such divine interventions a violation of individual liberties as well as a divine paternalism ill-suited to our human initiatives and autonomy?

Physical evil, then, really does exist, and, in humans, it is, very often, one of the consequences of sin. However, this physical evil is not really an obstacle preventing our self-realization; on the contrary, after the fact of sin itself, it is the principal thing that prods us to moral awareness. The principal sin of man, in effect, is the pride by which he tends to make a god of himself, acting as if he had no responsibility to anyone except himself. However, suffering can cure this kind of pride by teaching man that, far from being a god in his own right, he is a weak and powerless creature who depends for everything on others.

Furthermore, suffering offers man the opportunity to expiate for his faults. Our natural human sense of justice—when it is not clouded over—accepts joyfully every opportunity to make reparation for our faults and failings. Anyone who breaks something while visiting a neighbor is only too happy to repair the damage, to pay for it, or to replace the broken object; he feels *demeaned* if he is denied the opportunity to make up for what he has done; a situation of inferiority or dependence is established if his neighbor merely pardons him with "pity", without allowing him the opportunity of becoming his neighbor's equal again by balancing the account.[29]

The greatest happiness that can come to a man who has sinned and owned up to his sin is to be given the chance to make up for it, to make reparation, and thus to restore his personal dignity, destroyed, or, at any rate, strongly corroded, by the sin. The reparation we impose on ourselves for faults that we have committed form and deepen our characters. Even Scripture remarks on how the one who has suffered nothing knows nothing.

Considering the way men are, can we imagine a world without suffering? Have we not seen in a Hitler or a Stalin the evil that can be done by men who are in a position to get away with what they do? Who has not experienced the difficulty of working for a boss or a superior who has never been ill and sees only "laziness" or "lack of interest" in the worker who slows down for any reason? Also, the sufferings of others bring us out of the shell of our egotism. Sometimes, too, we realize the gravity of our own faults when we see their effects upon others; the alcoholic who has refused to face the fact of his condition and to seek a cure is sometimes brought to his senses only by seeing the effects of his drinking on his children.

Of course, none of these results is inevitable. It happens only too often that, as a result of human malice, the best of remedies can actually become worse than the diseases they are designed to cure. The child who richly deserves correction may nevertheless come to hate his parents for correcting him. The man whose trials have been too great for him may end up cursing God. But even in these cases we must judge about good and evil as they occur in the world we actually live in, not as they might be in an ideal world that does not exist and never will exist. The capacity that man has to sin—which is nothing else than the capacity to abuse the liberty God gave him—provides him with the power to use what is best in him to do harm. If a wicked and perverse man is prepared to use his faculties such as intelligence, will power, imagination, memory, or manual dexterity to commit a crime, how much more likely is he to abuse even the punishment that could correct that corruption of his best gifts! Certainly God could prevent all this by suppressing human freedom. He could also do away with suffering entirely. Would the world necessarily be a better place?

The Law of the Cross

The law of the cross, standing at the center of Christianity, brings a much more satisfying answer to all these abstract considerations. The poet Charles Baudelaire speaks of:

> God, who allowed suffering
> As a divine remedy for all our impurities . . .
> (Charles Baudelaire, *The Flowers of Evil*, "Benediction")

But the same God has Himself undergone all that same suffering. He made human suffering His own and, thereby, divinized it.

The Dominican theologian Thomas de Vio, called Cajetan (1469-1534), who had nothing of the sentimentalist about him, nevertheless wrote that in assuming our nature, Jesus, the Word of God made man, divinized in and through His human nature everything good that exists in the world; by accepting all the evils and indignities of our condition—solitude, rejection, calumnies, incomprehensions, crucifixion and burial in a tomb—Christ divinized even the evil that exists in the world (except sin!).

In and through Christ, the evil that exists in the world changes its nature; it loses its purely negative value as expiation, correction and reparation and takes on a positive, redemptive value. Henceforth, every man who unites his sufferings to those of Christ works alongside Christ for the redemption of the world. Not only does such a man "make up all that has still to be undergone by Christ for the sake of His body, the Church" (Col 1:24); he also prepares himself, by sharing Christ's sufferings (Rm 8:21) and helps prepare the universe at large, for that passage from "slavery to decadence to enjoy the same freedom and glory as children of God" (Rm 8:21) of which St. Paul speaks.

This is why even the sufferings of innocent children are profitable for Christianity. This is why, following Jesus Who described His own cross as a "lifting up" (Jn 12:32), St. Paul can rejoice and even "boast" (Rm 5:3) of his sufferings. This is why the early Christian martyr, St. Ignatius of Antioch, could tell the Roman Christians that they need not try to persuade the authorities to spare him from being delivered up to the wild beasts in the arena, since, as he wrote,

> If I suffer, I shall be emancipated by Jesus Christ, and I shall be reborn in Him (St. Ignatius of Antioch, *To the Romans*, IV.2).

Finally let us add—for it is impossible to say everything on such an inexhaustible subject as suffering—that by the power of Christ the man who suffers is torn away from the worst of his torments: his solitude. About this it has been aptly remarked that "we suffer and die alone." It was in one of his "Prayers for the Sick" that Blaise Pascal wrote the lines that follow; they sum up the entire Christian doctrine on suffering and death and demonstrate what an infinite gulf lies between the law of Karma and the law of the cross:

> Since only that is pleasing to God which has been offered to Him by You, Lord Jesus, unite my will to Yours, and my sufferings to the ones You suffered. Let my sufferings too become Yours. Unite me to You; fill me with Yourself and with Your Holy Spirit. Come into my heart and soul in order to endure my sufferings and to continue to endure in me what remains to be suffered of Your sacred passion that You

complete in Your members until the perfect consummation of Your Body. Filled with You, may I cease to live and suffer myself; let it be You Who live and suffer in me, my Savior! Thus, by sharing a tiny part of Your sufferings, may I be entirely filled with the glory that You merited through them and that You share with the Father and the Holy Spirit, forever and ever. Amen (Prayer IV).

The solution that Christianity brings to the problem of suffering is unique. Not only does Christianity explain *why* there is suffering; it also provides a real remedy for real suffering. Not only does it transform suffering into a positive value, but it also provides the strength to endure it; it provides the presence of a God Who Himself endures *in* and *with* suffering mankind. Finally, this divine infusion into our sufferings carries through to the end; it accompanies our death and burial, the final degree of our degradation at the hands of the forces of evil.

When we consider the true meaning of suffering in the Christian context, it becomes evident how radically out of place the doctrine of reincarnation would be in any Christian system.

Jesus suffered "once and for all" (Heb 9:26), and it is in and with Him that the Christian also suffers and dies "once and for all"; hence the Christian has no need of a series of other existences and deaths in order to benefit from the salvation that Jesus has procured for him at such a price:

> Since men only die once, and after that comes judgment, so Christ, too, offers Himself only once, to *take the faults of many on Himself*, and when He appears a second time, it will not be to deal with sin but to reward with salvation those who are waiting for Him (Heb 9:27-28).[30]

Footnotes

27. Read Text IX in the Appendix.
28. Oscar Wilde may mean here that a too arduous life, a life without pleasure can destroy the beauty of the human body. We should not forget, however, as Wilde himself demonstrated in his novel *The Picture of Dorian Gray*, that the pursuit of pleasure can also rapidly destroy the beauty of the human body.

29. He who pardons is thereby magnified, while he who is pardoned feels demeaned. This is why, in a not dissimilar situation, St. Vincent de Paul always tried to convince the poor he was helping of how much he needed *them*. They would thus not be humiliated by having to take what he gave them.
30. Read Text XI of the Appendix.

IV

FUNDAMENTAL CHRISTIAN ESCHATOLOGY

Summary. The finality of heaven and hell. The illusion of expecting conversion from multiple reincarnations. Purgatory and Limbo. Do the dead "sleep" or do souls live on with God in love?

We must not deceive ourselves: many Christians today are sympathetic towards the doctrine of reincarnation. Why? Because they see in it the means of escaping from the *fires*, whether those of Purgatory or those of Hell.

Christianity teaches that the soul's destiny is definitely decided at the moment of death; that, from this moment, there is no going back on the destiny that is in store. In such a stark perspective as this, it is understandable why some might prefer the doctrine of reincarnation which would provide the assurance that one had millions of existences to live through in which one might hope to modify anything as stark as final judgment.

One of our contemporaries, the Rosicrucian, Master Raymond Bernard, brought out on Canadian television one of the reasons why reincarnation ought in justice to be considered a possibility (just as the existence of inequality related to caste dramatically raised the same question of justice in the Indian context). How is justice served, Master Barnard asked, if a Christian who has lived a wholly virtuous life is irremediably condemned to hell because of a mortal sin committed at the end of his life? For that matter, how is justice served if a newborn child dying immediately after baptism merits eternal happiness in heaven without having to undergo any of the hard tests of our earthly existence?

I think that I have already provided the reply to this question in citing the parable of the landowner seeking laborers for his harvest. No Gnosticism can accept this parable, of course, because Gnosticisms leave out of account both divine *grace* and divine *pardon*. For this reason, it is necessary to examine Christian eschatology more closely on these precise points as well as looking at the differences between the doctrine of reincarnation and the doctrine of the resurrection.

The Finality of Heaven and Hell

In a well-known passage from the Gospel according to St. Matthew, Jesus has revealed to us the secret of the final destiny of human beings:

> When the Son of Man comes in His glory, escorted by all the angels, then He will take His seat on His throne of glory. All the nations will be assembled before Him and He will separate men from one another as the shepherd separates sheep from goats. He will place the sheep on His right hand and the goats on His left hand. Then the King will say to those on His right hand, "Come, you whom my Father has blessed, take for your heritage the Kingdom prepared for you since the foundation of the world . . ." Next He will say to those on His left hand, "Go away with your curse upon you, to the eternal fire prepared for the devil and his angels." . . . And they will go away to eternal punishment, and the virtuous to eternal life (Mt 25:31-46).

There is no necessity for me to discuss here all the concrete details with which successive generations of Christians have embellished the ideas of "heaven" and "hell;" these imaginative conceptions arise out of a human need to represent invisible realities by means of visible pictures. But that heaven is not literally a "banquet" should scarcely have to be argued; nor that hell does not necessarily include all the tortures that the Greeks and Romans ascribed to their Tartarus (many of which were appropriated by the Christian imagination as a matter of fact). What is quite certain, though, is that Jesus Christ did not die on the cross, as He is universally understood to have done in fact, in order to save us from nothing at all; nor did Jesus command us to take up our crosses in turn and to follow Him only in order that, in the end, all roads might lead to heaven anyway. Jesus is scarcely indifferent to whether we hear, or do not hear, His Word; or whether we do, or do not, put it into practice.

Let us therefore attempt to draw out of His teaching on the subject matter at hand what is quite plainly contained in that teaching, without, however, getting bogged down in minute details.[31]

One thing that is clear from the Gospel text that we have just quoted is the irremediable character of the decision made at the time of our exit from this life. There is no question of any sojourn of ours in some intermediate realm, either of light or darkness, from which we might then return to this earth through reincarnation. Another Gospel passage confirms this truth. Abraham, speaking to the unfortunate rich man in hell, says to him that

> . . . between us and you a great gulf has been fixed, to stop anyone, if he wanted to cross from our side to yours, and to stop any crossing from your side to ours (Lk 16:26).[32]

In this perspective, the New Testament's frequent exhortations to men to make the right choice since it will bind them eternally are most understandable: "Repent, for the kingdom of heaven is *close at hand*" (Mt 4:17). This "closeness" of the kingdom is an indication that it should be entered on immediately, that opportunities to enter will not be available forever. St. Paul makes the same point: "*Now* is the favorable time; *this* is the day of salvation" (2 Cor 6:2). Those who fail to take advantage of the occasions offered are like the foolish virgins of another parable, knocking in vain at the door where the wedding guests have assembled (Mt 25:12).

Another consideration can help us understand this point about the finality of heaven and hell. The very idea that the additional time for the soul furnished by various reincarnations automatically helps the soul is not well taken; this additional time might simply prolong the soul's *trial*, without adding to its chances for salvation. Here I cannot resist citing a Jewish parable commentary current in Palestinian synagogues around the time of Jesus; the commentator imagines King David at prayer, importuning God as follows:

> Lord of all, why do we speak of "the God of Abraham, the God of Isaac, and the God of Jacob," and not of "the God of David?" God replied: "Because I tested them; I haven't yet tested you." So David said: "Test me, Lord, and probe me" (Ps 26:2). God replied: "I will tempt you then. More than that, I will do something for you that I never did for them; I will let you know that it is with the sin of adultery that I am going to tempt you!"[33]

Even with this advance warning nothing was gained. When, shortly afterwards, David saw Bathsheba at her bath, he succumbed in spite of the warning, and thus completely failed the test.

Those who imagine that an indefinite number of reincarnations would necessarily be beneficent for the soul should reflect on this little story. Christians should provide the proofs of their good intentions in this present existence. If it is so difficult to stay on the straight and narrow path for a single week, how would it be any easier to do so through numerous new existences?

We may add another thought, drawn from our common modern experience. The history of the world provides us with few examples of really saintly lives. Sometimes we may even wonder whether humanity has really made much real progress on the moral plane. What century has perpetrated more violence, cruelty and injustice than ours? Can we argue from our modern experience that reincarnation would really contribute to any progressive amelioration of the human race? Only those fetched by the idea of progress can really plausibly imagine that a soul could pursue successive reincarnations from one galaxy to another in bodies successively more pure and ethereal. Impartial observers, for their part, will legitimately wonder why a criminal, for example, could be transformed into a better man in successive reincarnations merely by *knowledge*. Behind the doctrine of reincarnation is the old desire of man to save himself without reference to God. Edmond Rostand, in his play *Cyrano de Bergerac*, has admirably expressed this idea in a line spoken by Cyrano himself:

> Maybe I won't climb very high,
> But at least I'll do it *by myself!* (Act II, Scene 8).

Man's original temptation remains, whether we think of Adam in the Garden of Eden or of modern man today: "You will be like gods" (Gn 3:5). Man's original temptation is to pretend to be the sole and unique cause of his own perfection, refusing to recognize his dependence on the God Who created him and Who alone can *re*create and save him by grace. This is, precisely, "the sin of the world." This is why Christianity emphasizes humility and a recognition of man's absolute dependence upon God, whether in his natural existence or in his supernatural existence in the order of grace. This is the opposite conception of the Freudian idea that the child, in order to achieve self-realization, must "kill" his own father; rather, the child must die to his own pretensions of self-sufficiency in order to allow himself to be renewed by the divine power working within him:

> . . . unless a man is born from above, he cannot see the kingdom of God (Jn 3:36).

> Whoever remains in me, with me in him, bears fruit in plenty; for cut off from me you can do nothing (Jn 15:5).

The modern world is still imprisoned in the trap of Descartes and his rationalist idea of God merely providing the initial impetus for the operation of the world. The modern world believes that, once launched in his existence, man can go on to achieve or merit on his own, even to the point of divinizing himself. The modern world does not want even to hear about the *love* that actually created man; only man's rights and privileges are recognized. Thus, when Master Raymond Bernard is scandalized by the entry of baptized newborn babies into heaven, without their having had to undergo any test, we can reply to him with the words that the great St. Thomas Aquinas used in replying to a similar misconception of Origen's:

> It appears that Origen did not see that when we give something, not in strict justice but out of liberality, there is no injustice if we give unequal things without regard for the diversity of merits; retribution is only due to those who merit it. God, however, as we have seen, made everything that has been made out of pure liberality and without any obligation to do so. Consequently, the diversity of creatures does not presuppose a diversity of merits
>
> (St. Thomas Aquinas, *Summa contra Gentiles*, II.44).

The laborers who were hired first thus have no complaint if those who were hired later in the day receive *as much* pay as they do. God is free to dispense His gifts as He sees fit.

The Illusion of Expecting Conversion from Multiple Reincarnations

Since we have touched upon the argument holding that reincarnation would give men the chance to become better, let us dwell for a moment on this line of thought. For ₊his argument to be considered valid, it would be necessary for men to be aware of the faults committed in a previous existence and to set themselves seriously to correct these faults in their current existence.

I am well aware that some claim the knowledge of a previous existence or existences. By means of hypnosis or other methods, they claim to know exactly why they have been reincarnated in the bodies of women or of manual laborers when they should have been destined for better things. Even supposing that such favored reincarnated subjects hypnotized or not, truly did have the knowledge they claim, this knowledge would still benefit only them. The rest of humanity, remaining ignorant, would still be condemned, like the mythical Sisyphus, to roll the same rock up to the top of the mountain, only to see it come tumbling back down again. How can the rest of humanity correct its faults, or amend them, if they generally cannot even be known?

St. Justin seized upon the weakness of Platonism on this very same point. Speaking of reincarnated souls, he asked:

> "Do they know, then, that it is for this or that reason that they inhabit the body they have, that they have sinned?"
> "I don't think so."
> "Well, then, it seems impossible for them to profit by their punishment. I would even say that they are not really being punished, in fact, if they don't know that they are!"
> (St. Justin, *Dialogue with Trypho*, IV.6-7).

Thus there is a grave illusion in expecting the moral betterment of humanity through multiple reincarnations. We need think only of our recidivists or habitual criminals. Are they better in proportion to the time they have spent in prison or to the number of their convictions? If it is replied that the fault for that lies in our defective prison system, it would still have to be shown that our world in general provides any greater possibilities for moral improvement than our prison system. Even a glance at the state of the world at any given time can scarcely be very reassuring in this regard. Since this question is of central importance in our study, we would do well to ask ourselves just how far the doctrine of reincarnation can really be justified on this basis.

Purgatory and Limbo

To the biblical concepts of Heaven and Hell, Christian eschatology has added those of *Purgatory* and *Limbo*. We should look more closely at these two concepts, especially since some Christians today have come to see in the doctrine of reincarnation a concept that is superior to the notion of any Purgatory, as explained by Catholic theologians.

As for the idea of Limbo, it originated in unorthodox, sectarian circles, but many Christian theologians came to accept it as a valid and necessary solution to the problem of what happened to children who died without being baptized. St. Augustine, in his battle with Pelagius, was obliged to lay down the doctrine of Original Sin along very strict lines; as a result, he even came to accept that unbaptized infants logically had to be damned. In spite of the authority enjoyed by this great doctor of the Occident, there was never a theological consensus favoring his position; the idea of infant damnation seemed pitiless and unjust. It seemed much more reasonable to hold that unbaptized infants, although they were incapable of entering the heaven where God manifested Himself face to face with the soul baptized and sanctified in Jesus Christ, could at least be gathered into a kind of "natural" paradise where they would enjoy a beatitude perfectly natural to man, if God had not summoned us to a higher destiny. These unbaptized souls would contemplate God through His works without being able to contemplate Him face to face. Today, of course, there is perhaps a majority of theologians who prefer to believe that the souls of all innocent children, baptized or not, are in fact saved through the merits of Christ, and, by a special mercy of God, do enter into a perfect eternal happiness.

The doctrine of Purgatory was logically deduced from the teaching of the Scripture that nothing stained or impure could enter into the presence of God:

> Be holy in all you do, since it is the Holy One Who has called you, and Scripture says: *Be holy, for I am holy* (1 P 1:16).

Thus it was believed that those who died before achieving the requisite sanctity must in some way be purified before definitively entering into the Presence of God. This process if realized after death is in ways not altogether clear to us. The guilt sinners bear, the shame they shoulder are obstacles to the blossoming of perfect love of God and neighbor. Traditionally, purgatory has been viewed as a state of ongoing expiation for sin. God's forgiveness of the sinner is infinite and constant but the sense of justice within the forgiven sinner himself demands some type of reparation be made for harm done to self and neighbor. This, in broad terms, is how Purgatory is conceived. I have not thought it necessary to provide an exact summary of the most traditional theological doctrine about Purgatory; such a summary is not necessary for our purposes or in order for us to consider now the question raised by some Christians today as to why the doctrine of reincarnation might not constitute a much better response to the theological questions that seemed to make the traditional doctrine of Purgatory necessary.

To this notion, I reply, first of all, by saying that, unlike the traditional doctrine of Purgatory, there is not the slightest indication anywhere in Christian revelation that reincarnation is even so much as a possibility. By itself this reply is a strong argument considering that, outside of the divine assurance backing up what has been positively revealed, all ideas on the whole subject are no more than conjecture and *supposition*.

Secondly, reincarnation must either take place back into the bodies we have now, or into another body. If it takes place back into the same body, it is not reincarnation but resurrection. If it takes place in other bodies, it seems to me to be flatly contrary to the doctrine of the resurrection, in which is surely implied the idea that the same body that participated in our good works (as well as in our expiatory sufferings) should also be recompensed by its own resurrection. If Purgatory were really to be realized by one or more reincarnations, another body would obviously be required in each case.

Thirdly, if it is while we are in the body that the "purgation" of the impurities rendering us unfit to see God must take place, then this purgation would have to be accomplished amid the temptations and miseries of this world and of our present life. When we look closely at the inhabitants of our planet, however, we do not get the impression that large numbers of them are seriously embarked on any kind of purification, either interior or exterior; it is to be feared, as I have already remarked, that a series of reincarnations back into this world would be as often harmful as helpful to the souls that had to undergo it.

Finally, it is obvious that we human beings, supposing we were reincarnated in fact, do not in general recall or know anything about our previous existences. How could we be expected to recognize and correct faults stemming from them better than we can recognize and correct our known faults stemming from the present, single existence we are living now as presupposed by the Gospel system?

To sum up: Christianity teaches that our entire destiny unfolds in the sight of God and in the course of a single existence. This present existence can be considered a time of "testing." By this I do not mean that God is playing games with us or that He would like to see us fall. Quite the contrary: God watches over us at all the moments of our existence and many times provides us with the opportunity to reveal the quality of our hearts. Indulgent with regard to those who have been given little, God requires more from those who have been given more. He sacrificed Himself on the cross for our salvation, and hence He tries everything in order to make more accessible to us that eternity whose doors have been opened to us at the price of such sufferings.

It follows that Purgatory does have to be conceived outside of any cycle of reincarnations.

Do the Dead "Sleep," or Do Souls Live on with God in Love?

In the last part of this chapter I want to touch upon a problem that is much discussed today by Christian historians and theologians.

The New Testament is utterly plain and lucid on the doctrines of Heaven and Hell and on the finality of each; it is much less clear about the state of those defunct souls awaiting their glorious resurrection in Jesus Christ "at the end of time." Taking these facts into account, certain writers have held that it was a traditional Christian belief that those who died in the place of Christ are somehow now "asleep" in Christ and will not awaken until the day of the general resurrection.

Here are some of the arguments adduced for this point of view: 1) the legend of the seven sleepers of Ephesus; 2) the repeated usage of the word "rest" *("requiem")* in the traditional liturgy of the dead; 3) the custom of representing the defunct lying down on the tombs of the Middle Ages; 4) the common habit of identifying "ghosts" with the souls in Purgatory, thus helping to give rise to the notion that only perfectly sanctified souls achieve the beneficent "rest" thought to be the condition of those awaiting the resurrection, while the more imperfect souls are compelled, as a sign of their miserable, and as yet undetermined condition, to wander through the world.

My personal reaction to these kinds of speculations is that they raise more questions than are answered by our traditional catechisms.

First of all, in the liturgy of the Holy Mass, Peter and Paul, all the saints, apostles and martyrs, have been invoked from very ancient times. This practice, it seems to me, points to the existence of a very general belief in the power of intercession of these saints; they were scarcely considered to be in some kind of "sleep of death" awaiting the resurrection if they were actively expected to intercede.

Secondly, the two most ancient parts of the Mass of the dead, the *Subvenite* and the *In Paradisum*, ask the holy angels, patriarchs and martyrs to conduct into heaven the soul of the person who has just died. It is hard to imagine how "sleepers" could acquit themselves of such a task.

The ancient faith concerning Jesus' descent into Hell, as represented in Christian art, strongly suggests the idea that He brought out all the saints of the Old Covenant and transported them to heaven. Would Jesus then leave the faithful who directly believed in Him in some kind of "sleep"?

On the cross, Jesus promised the Good Thief that the latter would be with Him in paradise henceforth; and the idea of paradise implied by this promise was scarcely a Jewish *Sheol* or realm of shadows, but a place of happiness.

For all these reasons, then, I conclude that the Church's traditional faith that the souls of the just enter immediately after death into a realm of light and life is much better established and compelling than such speculations as we have been considering. Such indications as can be adduced pointing to a "sleep" of the dead awaiting the resurrection are as likely as not merely the mistakes of some past generations of Christians about what is truly entailed in revelation.[34]

Footnotes

31. Included in the Conclusion of this book is a section containing some basic questions and answers on the doctrine of reincarnation which throw further light on the doctrines discussed here.
32. St. Irenaeus of Lyons has produced an admirable commentary on this parable which, according to him, teaches "not only that souls do live on but that they do not pass from one body to another." Indeed, they "retain certain characteristics of the body that were theirs"; they "remember the works that they carried out in life." Finally, "each category of soul is transported to its appropriate place, even before the general judgment" (St. Irenaeus, *Exposition and Refutation of Gnosticism*, II.34.1).
33. I ran across this quaint little commentary in the *Kommentar zum Neuen Testament* by H.L. Strack and P. Billerbeck, on Matthew 6:13, "Lead us not into temptation."
34. Read Text XII in the Appendix.

V

REINCARNATION AND RESURRECTION

Summary. Belief in bodily resurrection. The soul separable from the body in reincarnation: proof through dreams; through "the shock of recognition;" through hypnosis. The reincarnation process in Hindu thought. The relationship between the body and the soul in Christian philosophy. The soul as the substantial form of the human composite. The creation of the soul and the animating of the body. Bodily resurrection: the survival of the integral human composite. The manner of bodily resurrection.

Belief in Bodily Resurrection

The most obvious point of opposition between the doctrine of reincarnation and Christianity is the latter's doctrine of bodily resurrection.

We have neither a rational explanation of, nor a cogent justification for, this doctrine; it is a truth of the faith that we derive from the teaching of Jesus:

> Do not be surprised at this, for the hour is coming when the dead will leave their graves at the sound of His voice: those who did good will rise again to life; and those who did evil, to condemnation (Jn 5:28-29).

The resurrection of Christ is the *image* and *prototype* of our resurrection. That is why St. Paul called Christ the *Beginning*, and then went on to add that

> . . . He was first to be born from the dead,
> So that He should be first in every way (Col 1:18).

That is why too, that born of Adam, we shall finish like Adam in the earth; but that, born of Christ according to the Spirit, we shall also rise with Him to a heavenly life:

> The first man, being from the earth, is earthly by nature; the second man [that is, Jesus] is from heaven. As this earthly man was, so are we on earth; and, as the heavenly man is, so are we in heaven. And we who have been modeled on the earthly man, will be modeled on the heavenly man (1 Cor 15:47-49).

As to the mode of this resurrection, St. Paul provides the following suggestions:

> Someone may ask, "How are dead people raised, and what sort of body do they have when they come back?" They are stupid questions. Whatever you sow in the ground has to die before it is given new life and the things that you sow are not what are going to come; you sow a bare grain, say of wheat or something like that, and then God gives it the sort of body that He has chosen: each sort of seed gets its own sort of body.
> Everything that is flesh is not the same flesh: there is human flesh, animals' flesh, the flesh of birds and the flesh of fish. Then there are heavenly bodies and there are earthly bodies; but the heavenly bodies have a beauty of their own and the earthly bodies a different one. The sun has its brightness, the moon a different brightness, and the stars a different brightness, and the stars differ from each other in brightness. It is the same with the resurrection of the dead; the thing that is sown is perishable but what is raised is imperishable; the thing that is sown is contemptible but what is raised is glorious; the thing that is sown is weak but what is raised is powerful; when it is sown it embodies the soul, when it is raised it embodies the spirit (1 Cor 15:35-44).

I do not want to go into all the antecedents and consequences of this very clear doctrine of the resurrection. I accept this doctrine just as the Church teaches it. Here I am trying to give it a more precise signification in the face of the challenge posed to it by the doctrine of reincarnation.

The Soul Separable from the Body in Reincarnation

The point of departure for belief in reincarnation is the postulate of the *autonomy* of the human soul; and the fact that it is believed possible for it to inhabit *different* bodies.

This postulate held by believers in reincarnation is, like all postulates, a "first principle," not demonstrated and not demonstrable, whose acceptance is necessary to establish any demonstration.

The ancient Hebrews were not tempted to establish such a dichotomy between the body and the soul because they believed that the principle of life resided in the blood; and they knew that blood quickly putrefied when it became separated from the body. It was for this reason that only at a relatively late date, and under the influence of Greek philosophy, were the ancient Hebrews prepared to talk about a true *immortality* of the soul.[35] This was not the case, however, with other ancient peoples who had a different conception of spirit and who were convinced that the soul could be separated from its body and resume its existence elsewhere, in other bodies.

Let us look at the proofs that were commonly advanced for this latter belief.

A. *Proof through Dreams*

We have already noticed the very ancient belief that the soul was separable from the body because, in dreams, it wandered off by itself. Is it not possible, in fact, to dream ouselves in Paris while we are sleeping in a bed somewhere in Quebec? Naturally, few occidentals would draw such a conclusion today. Aristotle in his time provided a natural explanation of how dreams arose in his treatise *On Dreams*, and I believe that the majority of modern psychologists would accept Aristotle's reasoning. There is nothing about dreams that obliges us to admit that the soul *abandons* the body during sleep, any more than it does when we mentally transport ourselves elsewhere during our waking hours by thinking about some distant scene. The power that we have to imagine ourselves elsewhere must not be confused with the reality of actually being transported elsewhere.

B. *Proof through "the Shock of Recognition"*

The phenomenon of "the shock of recognition" is described for us in dozens of different treatises. A man will arrive at a place where he has never been and, suddenly, he will be seized with the very strong impression that he has been there before. Since it could not have been during his present existence, he concludes that it must have been during a previous existence. From this conclusion, it is just one more step to hold that the soul can exist apart from the body, and, indeed, that it has so existed and that some can even bear witness to this previous existence.

The philosopher Henri Bergson, in his book *Mind Energy*, has devoted an interesting study to the phenomenon of "the shock of recognition:"

> In reality, this phenomenon is a unique effect produced by the mind as if it were a "memory of the present." It rises up out of the subconscious, and it seems to be a memory because a memory is an experience so distinct from an immediate perception, and so this phenomenon seems to be too; but it cannot really be a memory because we all know that we cannot live twice the very same moment in our lives.
>
> Since beginning to study this phenomenon, we have tried numerous times to get ourselves into the same state of mind described by those who have noted the experience; in this way we hoped to induce it experimentally in ourselves.... A requirement for really accomplishing this is to remove ourselves to the scene of a place that is not only new to us but one that is out of the ordinary for us as far as our habitual existence is concerned. It could be, for example, some

spectacle watched while on a trip, especially if the trip were an unplanned one. The first condition of a true shock-of-recognition experience would be a specific kind of "surprise" that I call "the surprise of being there at all." This particular kind of surprise has to be supplemented with a feeling closely related to it, namely, the feeling that *the future is somehow closed off*, that the experience is somehow detached from everything else at the same time that we are attached to the experience. To the extent that the two feelings, the "surprise" and the "closed off-ness," penetrate each other, reality loses its solidity and there is added to our perception of the here and now something else from "behind." Is it truly a memory of the present? It is hard to affirm exactly, but we are certainly on the way to duplicating the experience of "the shock of recognition"; little would be required to duplicate it exactly (Henry Bergson, *Mind Energy (L'Esprit Spirituelle)*, PUF, Paris, 1959, pp. 923 and 928).

To these observations we may add what Bergson also underlines, namely, that persons who are victims of the illusion of having already seen or experienced something they are currently seeing or experiencing are often suffering from a pathological condition, whether temporary or permanent. From such conditions it is scarcely possible to "prove" that the soul, in fact, is separable from the body and able to be reincarnated elsewhere.

C. *Proof through Hypnosis, Transcendental Meditation, etc.*

In this category we must also place the claims made by some of having died and brought back from the beyond some extraordinary knowledge and experience.

It is difficult, if not impossible, to test such claims, one way or the other; it is certainly difficult to take them at face value unless one is just waiting to be duped.

Already in his time Pythagoras was claiming that he could remember being a hero at the time of the Trojan War, being a prince elsewhere at a later date, and so on. It is amazing that he could never remember being a caterpillar or a stevedore or anything of that sort. There are to be found all sorts of people who claim to be Christ or the Virgin Mary or the Pope or Napoleon; but they are in psychiatric wards. We don't have to believe them just because they make their claims!

When a man is under hypnosis, he is unusually sensitive to suggestions and, moreover, to suggestions made by the slightest change in the hypnotist's tone of voice. In this fashion, he is apt to recall practically anything at all, and what it is can even depend upon how well he has dined before the seance. . . .

Similarly, a man on drugs or in the state induced by transcendental meditation can be visited by some very strange visions. The same is true of a man with a high fever or one anesthetized, or a drowning man, or one who has been stunned—all of these can under certain circumstances experience strange feelings of wellbeing, pass in review in the course of a second their whole past life, suddenly recall things long forgotten, and so on. But none of these things constitutes any proof that anybody has in fact experienced another world.[36]

Some memories, of course, are truly remarkable. There are cases on record of people under hypnosis speaking Swedish or German from having heard it spoken before them in childhood, or sung to them in rhymes or lullabies, by servants or others. Other people have demonstrated their ability to describe the room of a medieval castle which they had read about as adolescents in Sir Walter Scott (who expended considerable efforts to provide an authentic medieval touch). Thus, readers of esoteric works can indeed describe fantastic things for us which in fact they have only seen in their *memories*, influenced by reading done long ago, and perhaps forgotten.[37]

We would, then, be imprudent and indeed naïve to take too seriously the revelations that arise from dreams, hypnosis, transcendental meditation, and similar things. If we had no more than such intangible and equivocal "proofs" to support our belief in the divinity of Jesus Christ, we could be considered as superstitious as readily as religious.

However that may be, the proof that the soul is indeed separable from the body has simply not been provided by all these "proofs." As a Christian, I *believe* that the soul is immortal; hence I also accept philosophical demonstrations which tend to confirm my belief. At the same time, I recognize that other philosophies, not illuminated by the light of faith, hesitate to pronounce on the subject. As was true of St. Thomas Aquinas, I understand their anxiety and respect their uncertainty on this score.

The Reincarnation Process in Hindu Thought

The curious reader may be interested in knowing more about the manner in which the reincarnation process was conceived in ancient India. To be more precise, let us mention the era of Shankara, who flourished around A.D. 800, at a time when the Indian conception was well developed. Certainly Shankara is not an official representative of the whole of Hindu thought. However, because of his genius and erudition, he is one of the best sources we have for the meaning of the Vedas and their systematization in the Vedanta.

Let us glance, first of all, at how the soul, at death, was conceived as quitting the body. What was said on this subject was not so much strange or bizarre as it was in fact simply based on a fairly careful observation of certain facts about the human dying process.

First of all, the senses became enfeebled; old people began to lose their senses of sight, hearing, taste, and the like. Thus, it was imagined that all sense activity (vritti) retreated towards the *consciousness* (manas). Then the consciousness itself became clouded. Only *respiration* (prana) then continued to testify to the presence of life in the failing body. Then respiration itself ceased, and only the *body heat* (tejas) continued to suggest that death was not yet utterly final.

According to this Indian conception, the senses, the consciousness, respiration and the body heat all flowed back into the "subtle body" which, attached to the soul, carried away what was vital in the old body—or, rather, carried away the "seeds" of a new body, seeds that would determine the moral character of the individual's next reincarnation.

The "subtle body," then, always remained linked to the soul

during all reincarnations; indeed the soul only became separated from it at the time of nirvana and of its final fusing with the great All; only then did the soul discover its perfect authenticity (the identity between the Self and God). The "subtle body" was thus the *vehicle* of the soul's transmigration. And this vehicle was conceived of as being of a material nature; the Indians could not imagine that life could exist without material support (sûkshman shariram). The majority of modern Gnosticisms echo this same concept and speak of the various "bodies" or "envelopes" which the soul must slough off in order to achieve perfect identity with God. We find a vestige of the same concept in the idea of a division of bodies into "hylic (corporeal), psychic and pneumatic" which St. Paul seems to have been familiar with (1 Cor 2:14; 15:44).

Now we have to look at how the soul was conceived as re-entering a body. Here the inspiration seems to have come from the analogy of the "return" of life each spring in the case of vegetation. Let us try to imagine this Indian concept.

While it resided in the realm of light on the moon, the soul was thought to be covered with a "humid body" given to it for its delight. But it was only a temporary body which disintegrated, leaving the soul with its "subtle body."

The "subtle body," in order to travel through sub-lunar space in turn had to take on a "spatial body," followed by a natural covering of *air, smoke, clouds* or *rain*.[38] Under one of these natural coverings, the soul returned to earth and passed into plants or vegetation; in this state the soul experienced neither pain nor pleasure. Then, when the plants or vegetation in which the soul resided were consumed by animals or men, the soul itself passed into the animal or human *semen*, and thus was positioned to assume a new body in the womb of a woman impregnated by that semen.

This was how the reincarnation process was conceived in Hindu thought. The system is certainly simple and coherent—and it is linked to the observation of many material facts, as I have already noted, and, indeed, in a way, it represents a remarkable scientific-type synthesis. Modern Gnosticisms, often basing their speculations on scientific facts, merely develop this original Indian conception: they see the soul as moving from planet to planet and galaxy to galaxy; but in their conception no really new element has been added that was not already present in the ancient Indian conception, and I do not think we have to dwell on this further.

The Relationship Between the Body and the Soul in Christian Philosophy

There was a time when, according to a certain school of thought in scholastic philosophy, attempts were made to distinguish or establish a contrast between *matter* and *life*. This unfortunate dichotomy led to regrettable consequences and some unnecessary confrontations between scientists and believers.

If there is a distinction or contrast to be made here, it should be made between *matter* and *spirit*.

It is impossible to deny that there exists that which we understand by the word "spirit." However, it is not possible without contradiction to speak of "spiritual matter" or "material spirit."[39]

Is there in man a "spirit" that is distinct from man's material body? The ancient Hebrews, who certainly should not have thought so considering that they thought that "life" resided in the blood, nevertheless also conceived of a *Sheol* where souls descended after death. The Fathers of the Church did not immediately accept the theory of Plato, widely accepted in the Mediterranean world of the time, according to which the soul was immortal *by nature*, precisely because it was "spiritual." St. Justin, writing as a philosopher, tended to hold that the soul was only "immortal" because God willed it so, not by its nature[40]—but perhaps St. Justin was here resisting the various gnostic conceptions that tended to identify the "I" with God. However that may be, the following passage from him is most interesting considering its author and the time that he wrote:

> Only God is unengendered and incorruptible—these are precisely the characteristics that make him God; everything else whatever is engendered and corruptible. It is for this reason that souls die and are punished; for if they were not engendered they would not sin [because they would be

God!]; they would not be imbued with folly; they would not be cowardly, bold; they would not will to pass into the body of a pig, a serpent, or a dog. . . . The soul partakes of life because God wills that the soul live; the soul would live no longer from the moment that God no longer willed it to live. Life does not belong to the soul in and of itself but only to the extent that the soul belongs to God (St. Justin, *Dialogue with Trypho*, Chapters 5 and 6).

Since I do not wish to get into an arid debate on this subject, I will content myself with reproducing here the view of a modern philosopher who also had exact scientific training, Henri Bergson, whom I have already cited. Bergson affirmed his conviction that the source of man's life is not in the body alone, nor does it depend solely upon the brain, but, rather, it has to be sought in another source, in that spiritual principle that believers call the *soul*. Here is what Bergson affirms on this subject:

Whoever might look into the inside of a functioning brain, survey the movement of atoms there and understand what they were doing, would undeniably learn something about what goes on within the spirit of man; but he would learn little of real importance. He would know just what we know from interpreting the expressions, gestures and bodily movements of others. He would know something about the state the soul was in, or where it was tending; everything else about it would escape him. With regard to the thoughts and feelings unfolding in the interior of the person's consciousness, this observer would find himself in the same situation as a spectator in a theater who sees all the actors distinctly and observes their movements and gestures, but who cannot hear a word of what they are saying! Or such an observer would be like the person who could perceive nothing of a symphony except the gestures of the conductor waving his baton. Physical cerebral phenomena are to thoughts, what this conductor's gestures are to the symphony being played. These phenomena trace the articulations that cause the music; that is all that they do. We will discover nothing of the superior functions of the spirit by looking beneath the cerebral cortex. The brain, apart from its purely sensory functions, has no other functions except to trace or reflect, in the broadest sense of those terms, the real life of the mind (Henri Bergson, *Mind Energy (L'Énergie Spirituelle)*, PUF, Paris, 1959, p. 871).

Many scientists today would accept Bergson's view. The human brain is assuredly a marvelous machine, a device of admirable precision and complexity; still it is nothing but an *instrument*, a tool, one that has to be utilized by a *master*, who directs it towards his ends and "programs" it for his purposes. And this master that directs the brain is, precisely, *spirit*; it is that spiritual part of us that Aristotle, for purely scientific reasons very different from those brought forward by Plato, held to be distinct and separable from our bodies:

> In the case of certain beings, their form does not exist apart from their composite substance, for example, the form of a house . . . But if form exists apart from composite things, this can only be in the case of natural beings. . . . As for knowing whether anything can exist after the dissolution of a composite being, this has to be examined. In the case of certain beings there would be nothing to prevent this. This would be the case of the human soul, for example, not the soul as a whole, but certainly, the intellect (nôus) (Aristotle, *Metaphysics*, Book 3).

The reason that Aristotle here affirms that the intellect, which he regards as the superior part of the soul, has to be sharply distinguished from the body, and, upon death, is separated from the body, is the fact that our spirit is capable of operations *which exceed the possibilities of matter*. Thus, for example, my body constrains me to occupy a certain space at a certain time. In my spirit, however, I am able to cross space and time at a speed greater than the speed of light and to inhabit either the past or the future. More than that, I can turn back upon myself perfectly, being aware of the fact that I am aware of the operations of my thought;

I can will to will, or refuse to will, and, at the same time, know that I am willing or refusing to will. It is impossible to conceive of anything material being capable of such operations; it is inconceivable for anything in the order of *quantity* to operate in the fashion of the human mind, and matter is composed of quantifiable parts.

Thus we Christians are in agreement with the believers in reincarnation when they affirm that the soul is separable from the body. But we differ from them when they go on to affirm that the soul can pass from one body to another; this latter affirmation would nullify the true role that the soul plays with relation to the body; for the soul remains the principle of the body's life and movements.

The Soul as the Substantial Form of the Human Composite

Although there has been no solemn definition of faith on the matter, the theory that the human soul is the *substantial form* of the human composite of body and soul has, as a practical matter, become a firm and necessary component of the Christian tradition; because it is the substantial form of the body for which it was created, the soul can only be tied to *that* body.

This is not, however, a simple concept. It is easy for us to accept the existence of purely *material bodies*; we see them all around us. It is almost as easy to accept the existence of *pure spirits* such as God and the angels. Indeed it was the philosophers who originally conceived of such spirits, judging them necessary to the equilibrium of the cosmos since they bridged the infinite distance that, otherwise, would have existed between man and God. What is mysterious and would be difficult to accept, however, if we did not have the concrete evidence for it always before our eyes, is the existence of such a composite being as man—*composed of both body and soul!*

Origen could not agree that a spirit could undergo a destiny of being attached to a particular body. Influenced by Platonism—and hence by Indian Gnosticism—he imagined that in some primordial time the spirits had somehow sinned and hence deserved to be closed up in bodies until the time of their deliverance by Christ. In this conception, this early Christian believer and martyr was simply led astray by his Hellenistic culture. The Bible provided no basis for his particular theory, and the true doctrine of the resurrection, for which as a believer he was willing to give up his life, in fact implicitly condemned his particular theory.

The Judeo-Christian belief is that God expressly created man as a composite being, both material and spiritual, who was called to be master of the material universe, exercising over it a dominion assigned to him by the Creator:

> Be fruitful, multiply, fill the earth and conquer it. Be masters of the fish of the sea, the birds of heaven and all living animals on earth (Gn 1:28).

It was not as a *punishment*, it was by free, unmerited *love* that God created man and confided his mission over to the material creation to him; God gave man a suitable nature to accomplish the mission given to him:

> What is man that you should spare a thought for him,
> The son of man that you should care for him?
> Yet you have made him little less than a god,
> You have crowned him with glory and splendor,
> Made him lord over the work of your hands,
> Set all things under his feet.
> Sheep and oxen, all these,
> Yes, wild animals too,
> Birds in the air, fish in the sea,
> Traveling the paths of the ocean (Ps 8:4-9).

The Creation of the Soul and the Animating of the Body

We have seen how the Indians imagined the transmigration of a soul from a realm of light on the moon back down into a material body. Let us now see how the Christian tradition has represented the coming of a soul into a body and the sealing of its union with the latter.

God gives to human *parents*, as secondary causes, the power to engender; it is the parents who procreate the body, the indispen sable locus for the creation of the soul. But it is God Himself Who *directly* creates the soul. Thus, in the Christian conception, divine intervention enters into all human generation; this is true on a purely natural plane, and is one of the fundamental causes of the greatness of human life. The Book of Genesis describes the prototype of God's creation of every human life; God takes much more trouble with the creation of man than with that of the other creatures; for them, God contents Himself with a word: "God said . . . and so it was." But for man, God *fashioned* him from the dust of the earth and "*breathed* into his nostrils a breath of life" (Gn 2:7).

The soul thus infused into the material body forms with it a *single composite*, a single substance. It is a gross error to imagine that the soul could pass from one body to another, as a hand might pass from one glove to another. My hand can pass from one glove to another because my hand in no way gives life to the glove it is in and does not form with that glove a single living substance. But my soul has no other life than that which it shares with my body. The soul is affected by the body it inhabits, as the body is affected by the soul inhabiting and animating it. I can conceive of nothing, however immaterial or spiritual, that I have not first derived from what my senses or my imagination have first perceived in the material world. My imagination and my memory (which are faculties of the *senses*) are yet affected by the work of my mind and spirit. It is for this reason that human imagination and memory go so far beyond what we find in animals.

Modern psychoanalysis has revealed to us the extent to which sensible experiences such as shocks or traumas can hinder or prevent the proper functioning of our intelligence. Modern parapsychology, if not our own experience, similarly demonstrates how mind or spirit dominates matter, and imposes its laws on matter. Good news will revive a man on the point of death; bad news or worry can turn a healthy man into a bed-ridden one. The union of the body and soul is not a fortuitous, happenstance type of thing; this union indelibly marks our personalities and indeed defines our personal "I" or self. Indeed, so true is this of the union of the body and soul that even believers in reincarnation were constrained to postulate the existence of the "subtle body" in order to safeguard the soul's individuality and integrity in its successive migrations!

Bodily Resurrection: The Survival of the Integral Human Composite

Because of the substantial union of the body and of the soul, human death is a mystery as great as human birth.

The first image that comes to mind about death is that of a plunge into "nothingness." It is only by means of my, material body that I came into the knowledge and enjoyment of the *material* world, and, indeed, into the knowledge and enjoyment of the *immaterial* world as well. Thus, in losing my body, it seems that "creation" itself is disappearing from in front of my eyes, as I disappear from in front of creation's "eyes." Without my soul, my body is only an inert mass, good for nothing. Without my body, my soul is nothing but a vague, formless, fluid entity for which I can hardly imagine a new existence by itself.

I am happy that philosophers and theologians are able to assure me that the soul separated from the body will nevertheless be able to think and to will. Faith similarly teaches me that the detached soul will be able to live with God in love (Ws 3:9). But is this the totality of my hope? Will this spiritual immortality satisfy all my longing?[41]

The doctrine of the resurrection, even at this level, seems to me much more adequate; only this doctrine completes my original faith in God's creation of man as a composite of body and soul.

For God did not create us to be angels or spirits; He created us to be human beings, that is, beings of a particular category designed to be links between the spiritual and material worlds. If this was God's *original* plan for us, why would He not carry it through to its *final* realization still?

But—some might ask—is this not itself an argument for reincarnation then? To some extent perhaps—but not in the final analysis. The doctrine of the resurrection of the body does not envisage the return of the soul into any body whatever, but rather the authentic taking up again by the soul of the original body with which it was endowed at the birth of the person and which God, by means of his omnipotence, will give back to it in a better condition.

This, then, is what we desire in our deepest selves: not, as St. Paul remarks, that we should lose our mortal bodies, which, after all, are ours, but rather that we should see them transformed and, as it were, immunized from the afflictions to which they are heir in this life—and to which our spirits are consequently also heirs:

> Yes, we groan and find it a burden being still in this tent, not that we want to strip it off, but to put the second garment over it and to have what must die taken up into life. This is the purpose for which God made us (2 Cor 5:4).

Thus, for Christians, the doctrine of the resurrection of the body bears testimony to the *fidelity of God* in His plan for man. Having created man as He did, loving Him as he does, having died on the cross to assure his final restoration as the master and sovereign of the material world (and, as such, the "image" of God Himself), God now wants to maintain man eternally in the role assigned to him, and it is for this reason that God will reconstitute man in the latter's integrity, both bodily and spiritual; and re-establish him as the master of a new heaven and a new earth that God's power, again, will reconstitute.[42]

The Manner of Bodily Resurrection

I recognize how primordial "dreams" or "myths" can appear to us to be chimerical and impossible. But what if we were pulled out of some cave where we had lived in total ignorance of the present world and its marvels to learn for the first time about the stars and planets, animals and plants that God has in fact created? And what if, at the same time, we learned of God's plan that as spiritual beings possessing bodies, subject to the conditions of both matter and spirit, we should be the masters situated at the summit of that universe? Would we believe it all?

I also recognize how difficulties with bodily resurrection have been greatly magnified. Some have even gone so far as to imagine that they were frustrating the divine plan for a bodily resurrection by cremating corpses and throwing their ashes into rivers—as if the divine Power could not reconstitute the bodies treated thus!

Once again, it is Blaise Pascal who has countered, at one stroke, all the objections that have been made against the doctrine of the resurrection:

> *Atheists.* What reason do they have for saying that it is impossible to rise from the dead? Which is more difficult? To rise or to be born in the first place? To create out of nothing, or to recreate what has already existed? To come into being for the first time or to be reconstituted? Habitual occurrence makes some of these seem easy, while the others seem impossible! What a facile, popular way of judging the matter!
>
> How can atheists speak so casually against the resurrection? Or against the Virgin's bringing Christ to birth? Which is more difficult—to create an animal or a man, or to procreate one? If they had never observed a species of animals, would they ever have guessed that it was impossible for them to reproduce without partners?" (Pascal, *Pensées*, Brunschvicq Edition, Fragments 222 and 223).

This is a true man of science speaking; he refuses to allow judgment based on simple personal prejudices on matters on which there is neither power nor means to make an objective judgment.

In the same way, Charles Peguy went after those who denied the immortality of the soul on the grounds that this constituted a "metaphysical" question. But, Peguy pointed out, the *mortality* of the soul was equally a metaphysical question. If it was metaphysics as such that they were rejecting, they could no more affirm the soul's mortality than its immortality.

Bodily resurrection, for Christians, is a matter of *faith*. A specialist in scriptural exegesis might tell us whether or not this doctrine is in fact taught in the Bible; a theologian can interpret the implications of the doctrine for the faith as a whole; a painter or poet, instructed by theology and by the Christian tradition, can provide us with a "felt" representation of the Christian belief. However, only a very obtuse person would attempt to establish such a belief by rational proofs—or would attempt to disprove it by purely rational means. It is a characteristic strong point of any truly cultivated spirit to understand what is, and what is not, subject to rational proof in any given discipline—and what method of demonstration is appropriate in each case.

However that may be, let us sum up and conclude these particular reflections by affirming that the doctrine of the resurrection contradicts both Gnosticism and the doctrine of reincarnation. It contradicts Gnosticism by denying that man will ultimately be "liberated" from his body; it contradicts reincarnation by denying that the same soul can inhabit a multitude of bodies. Let us carefully consider the precise language of the Bible on these points:

> . . . we are not going to die, but we shall all be changed. This will be instantaneous, in the twinkling of an eye, when the last trumpet sounds. It will sound and we will be raised, imperishable, and we shall be changed as well, because our present perishable nature must put on imperishability and this mortal nature must put on immortality" (1 Cor 15:51-53).

Or, let us consider the following even more apocalyptic vision:

> The sea gave up all the dead that were in it; Death and Hades were emptied of the dead that were in them; and everyone was judged according to the way in which he had lived . . . and anybody whose name could not be found written in the book of life was thrown into the burning lake (Rv 20:13-15).

This language is highly symbolic, of course, but by means of its symbolic character, it conveys a real teaching. When a boss says to one of his employees—if bosses still have such power today so to say—"Get your gear together and get out," the employee can perhaps understand the meaning of "gear" in different ways, but unless he is a complete idiot, he will hardly imagine that the boss is inviting him to dinner. And so it is with the Gospel texts just quoted. We can understand in a number of ways what the terms and imagery used mean; but we can hardly derive from such texts the idea that what will happen to us at the end will be repeated over and over again dozens of times, or that we are destined to carry on a human existence indefinitely.

The warning of Jesus inevitably comes to mind here:

> . . . stay awake, because you do not know the day when your master is coming (Mt 24:42).

For the day when the master does come will be characterized by an irrevocable decision:

> And they will go away to eternal punishment, and the virtuous to eternal life (Mt 25:46).

We may remark, in moving to our conclusion, that this latter text merits great consideration. Going back to primitive texts for the purpose of making a closer study of them concerning our last end, certain theologians have affirmed that for those who have done evil there will not really be any "eternal punishment" but purely and simply a "death," or total disappearance. They support this affirmation with Rev 20:6 which speaks of a "second death," this one to be eternal, and they deduce from this, contrary to Mt 25:46, which ought to be sufficiently clear, that there will not really be any eternal punishment for the damned.

The last word has not yet been spoken in this particular debate. For my part, I would hate to see a "sweet condescension" for the plight of sinners, blind anybody to the plain teaching which the Church proposes to us through her sacred books as coming from the Master Himself.

For one thing is certain. We read in the very same passage of the Book of Revelation the following, in full:

> Then Death and Hades were thrown into the burning lake. This burning lake is the second death, and anybody whose name could not be found written in the book of life was thrown into the burning lake (Rv 20:15).

From the entire passage it is plain that the author of the Book of Revelation is taking pains to make sure that nobody misunderstands what he means by the second death, namely, the sojourn of the damned in Hell, or the "burning lake." In this he agrees with Jesus, as reported in Mt 25:41:

> He will say to those on His left hand, "Go away from me, with your curse upon you, to the eternal fire prepared for the devil and his angels."

Why an "eternal fire" if the damned are caught up and consumed in it in an instant? I am quite prepared to admit, once again, that we are dealing with *symbols* here. Nevertheless symbols have an underlying meaning by their very nature, and it is doubtful that Holy Scripture intended by these particular symbols the exact contrary of what they appear to signify.

What the Christian revelation teaches, then, is a resurrection for all men without exception, but a resurrection that will be glorious for some, but painful and shameful for others. St. Irenaeus was able to write about it in his *Demonstration of the Apostolic Preaching* (Chapter 1); he too employed a symbolical style of expression, but he in no way contradicted what I have been saying. Thus:

> For those who see, there is only one way—it goes up, illuminated by celestial light. For those who do not see, there seem to be many alternative ways, none illuminated and all heading in different directions. The true way leads to the kingdom of heaven where man is united with good; the other ways lead to death, where man is separated from God.[43]

Footnotes

35. This assertion does not tell the whole story, however, for the ancient Hebrews also conceived of a *Sheol* inhabited by the *souls* of the dead.
36. We should take note of the fact that our dreams or nightmares normally take place at the beginning or the end of our periods of sleep: hence they do not necessarily reveal what has been experienced in a deep sleep.
37. I have looked at "The Edgar Cayce Story on Reincarnation" (in *Many Mansions*, by Gina Cerminara, New American Library, 1967) and was not

surprised to find psychoanalytic interpretation aiming to establish that certain human behavior could be ascribed to traumas in a previous existence. I have no confidence at all in such assertions. Psychoanalysis has its own sphere of certitude—as well as its limits. When a mother points out to me how her son makes the same gestures as his father, whom he never knew, I am suitably impressed by the phenomenon; but I do not invoke reincarnation to explain it because the boy's father only had a *single* soul (and he was still alive when his son *began* his existence).

38. The belief in the return of souls to earth in raindrops is a very ancient one and can be found in various civilizations.

39. St. Paul adopts a common gnostic expression, although he transforms the sense of it, when he writes that what is sown embodies the "soul" but when "it is raised it embodies the spirit" (1 Cor 15:44); nobody has yet found a better word to describe a "glorious" (resurrected) body.

40. Christian writers of the second century spoke of *corruptible* and *incorruptible* beings in the sense that we now speak of *necessary* and *contingent* beings, that is, beings that either had to be or could possibly not have been. On this point, *see* G. Larger, *Étude sur le Livre de la Sagesse*, Paris, 1969, who attempts to explain how the author of the Book of Wisdom, influenced by Greek thought, dealt with the immortality of the soul.

41. There is one Gospel text on the resurrection that should rightly astonish us, one that I have not mentioned up to now; it is the discussion between Jesus and the Sadducees (Mt 12:23-33; Mk 12:18-27; Lk 20:27-38). In my opinion, what we read in these Gospel accounts has reference more to the survival of the soul after death than it has to the final resurrection properly speaking (although that is implied). Let us focus on Jesus' principal reasoning: "God is God, not of the dead but of the living" (Mt 22:32). The Old Testament idea echoed here is the idea of God as the source of all life; whoever becomes separated from God thereby dies. The just, who have lived *for* God, thereby *cannot* die, attached as they are to God Who gives life.

42. On this point, let us take another look at the great St. Ireneaus, in his *Exposition and Refutation of Gnosticism* (V.6.1): "The flesh . . . by itself, is not the whole man, but only his body. . . . The soul, by itself, is not the whole man either; nor does the spirit [i.e., superadded grace] constitute man. It is the union in communion of all three of these realities that constitutes the whole man. . . . Why would St. Paul envisage an integral conservation of these three distinct realities pending the coming of the Savior, as he does in 1 Th 5:23, if he had not known that all three were to be restored and reunited; and that for all there would be one and the same salvation?"

43. Read Text XIII and XIV in the Appendix.

CONCLUSION

In the domain of religion, it is possible to say about the doctrine of reincarnation what we might say about the Ptolemaic theory in the domain of astronomy: both are admirable syntheses containing many of the observations and discoveries of man down through the ages. Without Ptolemy, in fact, Copernicus would never have been possible. Without the doctrine of reincarnation, many points touching upon the survival of man after death might have remained in the dark; and consequently even the doctrine of the resurrection might have found acceptance more difficult.

Belief in reincarnation reassured men about their own personal survival, and that was a considerable accomplishment. This belief exerted a profound influence on the consciences of many men by asserting that the conditions of their future reincarnations would depend upon their behavior in this life. It helped many men to transcend the level of an inferior religiosity which saw only magic in religion and promised heaven without any other conditions than ritual observances and sacrifices, damning those who failed to wash their hands in a certain way or in the proper circumstances. The belief in reincarnation, if I may say so, reestablished a spiritual justice, applicable impartially to all men, whether the weak or the strong, under a changeless law of Karma from which the gods themselves could not escape.

But it was precisely at the moment of the doctrine's most rigorous and consistent development—at the time of the appearance of the Upanishads—when it became rigid and inhuman. The human survival guaranteed by the doctrine was no longer exactly a blessing; it was a continual returning back into this world, where moral progress was in no way facilitated. One's very ignorance of his past existences discouraged reform and amendment or a change of heart; the absence of divine grace or pardon pointed only to possible new falls rather than encouraging any effort to amend one's life. Each person can say to himself that he is miserable because of his sins in a previous existence, but since he has no real or precise knowledge of what these sins might have been, he is unable to guard against them in the future.

Certainly these reincarnated souls could always devise an ethic, imagining that such and such behavior would improve their future prospects. But their ideas about the sort of behavior that would be necessary would not really be founded on anything. No one could say that these ideas were not the correct ones to insure most favorable reincarnations; no one could say that they were either. Everything boils down to the gratuitous assumption that if we have to live our lives over again, we ought to be able to live them better the next time around. To affirm this may be flattering to our amour-propre, but is it a well-founded affirmation in fact? Perhaps we will succeed in avoiding this bit of foolishness or that particular fault next time—knowing what we have had to pay for them. But others? How many times in our lives, trying to avoid one particular vice or sin, have we not fallen into another, and perhaps a worse one? Would we be more saintly if we had an extra hundred years to live, when we know very well that we have not even been able to live the previous week without fault in spite of our most ardent desires to do better!

The principal defect of the system of reincarnation is that it both fails to take into account the true misery of man—and the true grandeur of God. We are asked to believe that the conversion of man's heart will be easier if only he is granted more time; that what is chiefly lacking for man's salvation is both enough time and sufficient *knowledge*. There is no sense of the distance between knowing the good and doing it, between recognizing the evil and avoiding it. There is no realization that the most difficult thing is not to choose the good over the evil, but to persevere in one's choice in a consistent manner and not to be turned away by new circumstances that arise. As St. Paul says:

> I cannot understand my own behavior. I fail to carry out the things I want to do, and I find myself doing the very things that I hate. . . . The fact is, I know of nothing good living in me—living, that is, in my unspiritual self—for though the will to do what is good is in me, the performance is not, with the result that instead of doing the good things I want to do, I carry out the sinful things I do not want (Rm 7:15-19).

What man longs for in his deepest being is not to be reincarnated but rather to be delivered

> . . . from this body doomed to death (Rm 7:24).

By *body*, St. Paul here does not mean merely the "envelope" of flesh itself, but rather the disorder that accompanies our entire present existence in the flesh and prevents a harmonious communion with ourselves and our neighbors.

The illusion of reincarnation is the conviction that man can save himself by his own powers and efforts; it is the conviction that man really has no need of God nor of anyone else to arrive at his own salvation; it is the belief that man can restore the *being* that he lost by sin and thus exercise over his own destiny the veritable power of a creator.

Once again I will leave it to Blaise Pascal to analyze the situation and draw out its meaning with his incomparable power to see into the essence of things:

> Some, considering nature incorruptible, others, considering it beyond redemption, could not avoid the trap of either pride or sloth, which are the two sources of all the other vices. . . . If they grasp the excellence of man without realizing his corrupt nature, they become proud; if they realize the infirmity of his nature without comprehending his dignity, they only avoid the vanity of the first group by

plunging into despair. From these attitudes arise Stoicism and Epicureanism respectively. . . .

Only the Christian religion has the cure for these two vices, not by chasing out one with the other, according to the wisdom of this world, but by chasing out both by the simplicity of the Gospel. For the Christian religion teaches the just whom it raises up to participate in the divine nature that even in this sublime state they still carry within themselves the source of their own corruption, and that it is this corruption that makes them all their lives subject to misery, error, sin and death; at the same time it teaches the impious that even they can receive grace from the Redeemer.

Thus Christianity consoles those it condemns and makes tremble those it justifies, tempering fear with hope in exactly the right measure by the double capacity it has to deal with both sin and grace. Christianity places man lower than reason does, though without despairing of him, but it also raises him infinitely higher than mere pride of nature does, though without puffing him up; by this double exemption from both intellectual error and moral failing, Christianity shows how it alone is really capable of instructing and correcting men (Pascal, *Pensées*, Brunschvicq Edition, Fragment 435).

I am well aware of how the law of Karma has ultimately been modified and softened in Indian religion. The Bhakti movement has attempted to associate the idea of mercy with the original rigorous system of justice. I am also aware that some Christians today have attempted to reconcile the doctrine of reincarnation with that of the resurrection, imagining, I suppose, that 2 + 2 might just as well add up to 3 or 5 rather than always to the vulgar 4 found in all elementary school textbooks. But I believe a more careful study of the whole question demonstrates that, once the Christian revelation was completed, the doctrine of reincarnation had nothing further useful to add in the religious sphere. If the salvation of man is first and foremost an affair of God Who saves us in Jesus Christ; if this salvation is a gratuitous gift of God rather than something merited; if it is far beyond the power or ability of men to effect on their own—if it is all these things, then what is the point of being endlessly reborn merely to obtain what, according to Psalm 127, God "provides for His beloved as they sleep"?

In any case, the doctrine of reincarnation is tied up with a system of thought seeking to liberate man from the horrible prospect of an *eternal return* upon the earth. The system of thought ushered in with the Upanishads—better known in the West under the name of *Gnosticism*—has provided a much more facile solution to the problem of human destiny. Gnosticism has thought that the human "I" or "self" is itself divine, by nature, and that all man's misfortune arises merely from his ignorance of the sublime truth of his own divinity; if only man did know this truth about himself, he could apply to himself these verses of the poet Lamartine:

> Courage, child, fallen from a divine race,
> You carry on your forehead the mark of your lofty origins;
> Anyone, seeing you, would recognize in your eyes
> A ray of light from high heaven.
> Come, assume the position of your first splendor
> Among the pure children of light and glory
> That God has wished to love
> With an outpouring of song of belief and love.
> (Alphonse de Lamartine, *Premières* Méditations,
> "Ode to Lord Byron")

The Gnostic often claims to be able to establish the truth of his claim by some such esoteric discipline as Yoga, under whatever form—Yoga Mantra, Yoga Tantra, etc. Once established in one of these disciplines as the means of escape, he rejects reincarnation as facilely as he rejects the resurrection. For him even reincarnation is just one more appearance or illusion (maya). As for the resurrection, it would condemn man eternally to the status of an inferior creature, subject to the influence of the stars and of the material world, according to this view.

In the course of this work, I have not, for the most part, attempted to underline how far Gnosticism is simply opposed to the Gospels, or how it simply negates the divine transcendence and makes perfectly superfluous the notion of both sin and grace. These things are essential to Christianity, which is centered upon the self-sacrifice of a God who died, gratuitously, in order to wipe sin out and give to men the *power* to become *children* of God. Hence it has to be clearly said that the gnostic solution to the problem of reincarnation is wholly unacceptable to Christians. Besides providing a solution to a problem that doesn't really exist—for there is no proof that there is any reincarnation or reincarnations—Gnosticism simply returns us back to the sin for which man was originally expelled from paradise, an expulsion which elicited the following ironic remark from the Creator:

> See the man has become like one of us with
> his knowledge of good and evil (Gn 3:22).

He is an impoverished man who imagines that it is sufficient to think that he is God in order to become God!

Thus, for the Christian, neither Gnosticism nor reincarnation should have any attraction. Either system involves a return to insufficient, outmoded religious ideas. Who wants to go back to the imperfectly expressed ideas of earlier religious gropings? Who wants to go back to Ptolemy after having studied Copernicus?

The only advantage there is for us to dwell on these ancient beliefs and convictions is the lesson of humility and gratitude we can derive from them: humility, because of our realization that we cannot, in fact, have any certainty arising out of our own knowledge or power concerning our final destiny; gratitude, for the action of God's grace and the realization that, in our blindness, God has had pity on us and has summoned us to a perfect hope, reminding us at the same time of the purpose of our earthly existence. All of these considerations only make more pertinent the words of Pascal that follow immediately upon the ones I quoted at the very beginning of this study:

> It is indubitable that the time of our life is but an instant;
> the state of death is eternal, for whatever nature we are

talking about; that all our thoughts and actions must take very different routes depending upon the state of that eternity; and that it is impossible to take a single step with sense and good judgment, except by regulating it through the truth that must be our principal subject (Pascal, *Pensées*, Brunschvicq Edition, Fragment 195).

QUESTIONS AND ANSWERS ABOUT REINCARNATION

NOTE: Having given quite a number of talks and lectures on reincarnation to diverse Quebec audiences, I have frequently gotten particular questions on the subject which I think useful to cover here since it could be that these same questions keep occurring to other people.

1. If reincarnation is not possible, how is it possible to explain the Incarnation?

Perhaps reincarnation is not metaphysically impossible: all I contend is that the doctrine contradicts what God has revealed to us in the Bible concerning the final destiny of man.

With respect to the Incarnation of the Son of God, this is a mystery belonging to an entirely different order than the question of the reincarnation of human souls. We do not believe, in fact, that the Son of God took a body in exactly the same manner as a human soul does. The Christian position on this subject is much more subtle. We believe that the Son of God assumed and attached to His person the particular human nature that, by His power, had been engendered in the womb of the Virgin Mary. From this it follows that in Jesus there are two natures: a perfect human nature, composed of a human body and soul; and a perfect divine nature. These two natures are united in the person of the Word of God.

We may add, since some may question me on this point, that the Indians, in their religion, speak also of *avatars* or of *bodhisattvas*, that is, of gods made men or of sages who voluntarily give up the blessing of nirvana to return back to earth in order to teach men the proper way to liberation. These conceptions, though, have nothing in common with the Christian doctrine of the Incarnation of the Son of God. The avatars are, in fact, as often as not, gods who have *sinned* and, themselves unable to escape the inexorable law of Karma, are reincarnated in order to expiate for their faults. These avatars can also simply be *demons* incarnate rather than gods, properly speaking. In fact, the Brahmins, in order to protect their followers from the Buddhists whom they regarded as heretics, taught that Buddha himself was a demon descended to earth in order to mislead men. As for the Bodhisattvas, admirable as they are in their concern for their fellow men, they are still conceived only as reincarnated men.

On this subject, which is perhaps of increasing interest, I would like to cite the conclusion of a recent book by Geoffrey Parrinder, *Avatar and Incarnation* (The Wilde Lectures in Natural and Competitive Religion in the University of Oxford, New York, Barnes and Noble, 1970, pp. 278-279):

> At the beginning of this book, reference was made to Aldous Huxley's assertion that the doctrine of the incarnation of God is found in most religions. It should have been apparent long since that this is not so. The Sufi mystics almost to a man rejected incarnation and many wandered in the deserts of monism. Mahayana Buddhism knew nothing of the idea of God, though it found substitutes in Buddhas and Bodhisattvas. The closest approach to Christian belief is the Avatar faith of Hinduism though it had little historicity and no real suffering. . . .
>
> Jesus reveals God in Incarnation, God in action, God in the perfect man, He shows the very nature of God, in love and suffering . . . Christ "emptied Himself" and lived and died on earth, and yet at the same time He is the eternal Word "in Whom all things consist" . . . .

The Word which was with God, whose life was the light of men, the true light lighting every man, who was in the world, came into his own, became flesh and dwelt among us. Divine law and right (dharma) were manifested in Avatars and Buddhas. Divine love and suffering were incarnate in Jesus Christ.

2. Everything in nature is reborn. Why would this not be the case with man as well?

The use of the word "reborn" here is rather broad. Trees, for example, are not really "reborn" in the spring; they simply continue their normal life which became dormant during the winter months. There are plants that grow new stems and flowers each year that disappear before winter; but their roots remain alive in the ground. When a plant or animal dies, it is *not* reborn; it is replaced by *others*, different from the original plant or animal even if born from them. It is clear, therefore, that we have to use the concept of being "reborn" with care, although it certainly can serve as an inspiration to thought. St. Paul himself employs it in this fashion to illustrate the resurrection, as does the early Letter of St. Clement of Rome.

Also, man *is* reborn in Jesus by baptism, according to the words of Jesus reported by St. John (Jn 3:3): "Unless a man is born again from above, he cannot see the kingdom of God." Man will also be reborn in a symbolic sense at the time of the final resurrection which will inaugurate an eternal springtime for the entire material universe.

3. Do we not have, in the case of diabolical possession, a spirit inhabiting a body not its own, and hence a form of reincarnation?

Assuming that we are dealing with a case of true diabolical possession, we must still understand that the devil does not *animate* the body being possessed but merely acts in and through that body as an external force, just as it is possible to act through the medium of a rope or a tool without being directly connected with the work one is carrying out. The same thing is true of a person under hypnosis; he acts under the constraint of the hypnotist, although he is certainly in no way "animated" by the hypnotist; nor is the latter "incarnate" in him.

In the majority of supposed cases of diabolical possession, nothing is produced but pathological phenomena. The possessed, like certain cases of hysteria, can deploy an astonishing physical energy and even exhibit signs of hysteria; can deploy an astonishing physical energy and even exhibit signs of levitation, telepathy, etc. Many today believe most of these phenomena can be explained by psychology or parapsychology. At the very least it is to be feared that an undue credence in certain actions as being those of the devil could be superstitious and could create a kind of collective hysteria about diabolical possession that could bring true religion into disrepute.

4. Certain people claim that they can remember their previous existences. Is this not a striking proof of reincarnation?

I have already replied in part to this question in the course of my expositions (Part Two, Chapter 5). I do not deny the good faith of those who make such claims. I only say that they are mistaken about the value of these kinds of recollections. It has been proved that dreams or nightmares do not occur during our deepest sleep, but rather either at the moment when we are falling asleep or at the moment when we are on the verge of waking. Similar visions of "another world"—for example, those experienced by the drowning or by patients being operated on—usually occur just as they are ready to regain consciousness.

I have also noted how some people have prodigious memories. Under hypnotism or sometimes by other means, they are able to repeat word for word descriptions of places that they have never seen except through reading or hearing sermons, etc. The case of the visions of Anna Catherine Emmerich and other mystics are very probably of this kind; what they tell us about the Passion of Christ are a reconstruction of elements from a prodigious memory or an enviable creative imagination. A man raised in an atmosphere where stories are constantly told about werewolves or will-of-the-wisps is all too likely to end up seeing such things. Readers of accounts of extra-terrestrial visitors are most likely, sooner or later, to be the ones to encounter such visitors. *We believe easily in what we hope for*, and, in cases of weakness or interior disequilibrium, we may even end up seeing and touching what we believe in and hope for.

5. *The New Testament says of John the Baptist that "with the spirit and power of Elijah, he will go before Him" (Lk 1:17). Elsewhere, the disciples ask Jesus: "Why then do the scribes say that Elijah has to come first?" (Mt 17:19). How can these texts be interpreted if there is no possibility of reincarnation?*

The Prophet Elijah played a decisive role in the history of the ancient Hebrews. At a moment when practically all of Israel seemed headed towards idolatry, he restored belief in One God. For this reason he remained the most popular of all the prophets, as can be seen in the frescoes of the Synagogue of Dura Europos executed two centuries after the birth of Jesus. There was a current of Jewish thought which held that there would be great temptations to impiety before the advent of the Messiah and that hence God would send a *new* Elijah to prepare a receptive people for the Lord so that they would be worthy to receive the salvation of God. Luke saw in John the Baptist this "other" Elijah, or this "new" Elijah, who would prepare the way of salvation for the people. It is hard to see how the reference to Elijah in his Gospel could possibly mean anything else. The Gospel text does not say that Elijah will come but rather that John the Baptist will precede the Messiah with the spiritual power of Elijah. He will not, therefore, be a reincarnation of Elijah, but another prophet animated with the same spirit and possessor of the same power as Elijah. There is an old saying in the Province of Quebec that such and such a one either has or has not, "the head of Papineau"—but the currency of this saying in no way proves that anybody ever really believed in a reincarnation of Papineau!

In spite of this, we must recognize that, in the popular belief—attested to by both Jewish and Christian iconography—there was an expectation that not only would Elijah return in person but that Enoch would return as well. But these returns were not understood as reincarnations. Because of the mysterious language of Scripture, the popular belief was that neither Elijah nor Enoch ever actually died; because of their sanctity, they were believed to have been taken up from the earth, bodies and all—a belief that perhaps explained the fact that there was not any tradition about their tombs. Since, according to Jewish belief, all men are mortal, it was imagined that from the time of their having been taken up, Elijah and Enoch were lodged in a special place near to God awaiting the time when they would redescend to earth to participate in the final messianic conflicts. In the course of these conflicts, it was expected that they would be killed, and thus finally die like all men (and participate in the resurrection). We must note about all this that it has nothing to do with reincarnation at all; nor do the popular beliefs on the subject really possess dogmatic value.

There is, however, one place where Jesus clearly delivers His opinion on the subject of reincarnation. I have already mentioned it. It occurs at the place where the disciples ask Jesus about the man born blind: " 'Rabbi, who sinned, this man or his parents, for him to have been born blind?' 'Neither he nor his parents sinned,' Jesus answered, 'He was born blind so that the works of God might be manifest in him' " (Jn 9:2-3). This reply is equivalent to saying: don't try to explain the existence of evil in the world by reincarnation!

Finally, on this same subject, let us recall the careful and jealous attachment the first Christians had to the teaching of Jesus; they condemned every deviation, every *heresy*; they rejected numerous apocalyptical writings by Gnostics trying to deceive the members of the Great Church, items with titles such as *The Gospel of Truth, Treatises on the Resurrection, The Apocryphon of John*, etc. Since this is the case, it is hard to understand how the early Church was simply *silent* on the doctrine of reincarnation if there is any truth in the idea that this doctrine possibly formed any part of the teaching of Jesus. The early Christians were never shy about proclaiming their belief in the resurrection; they underwent martyrdom in order to affirm that the risen Christ was the Son of God. How is it that there is no authentic Christian text accepted by the early Church that ever makes mention of reincarnation as one of the doctrines accepted among orthodox Christians? Remember that the pagan atmosphere in which the early Church lived was saturated with the idea of reincarnation, and, if the Christians had believed it, it would have constituted another bridge to the pagan world they were trying to convert. Let us not therefore give credence to any efforts to claim that Christians ever believed in reincarnation. Everyone remains free to be a Christian or not to be one, but no honest person or sincere researcher should ever permit himself to falsify his sources in order to support his own beliefs in such matters as these.

6. If you reject the idea of substituting reincarnation for the doctrine of Purgatory, what then is your idea of the nature of Purgatory, and what is the point of Masses for the dead?

Let us recall, first of all, that the "flames" of Purgatory, like the various forms of "torture" which the Christian imagination have assigned to the damned are *symbols*. We do not know *exactly* what the punishment of the damned will be; we only know that, as the saying is, "happiness will pass them by," since they will have lost the vision of God—and that itself is already the worst of punishments.

Let us also recall that the soul, once separated from the body, no longer exists in the *time* of this world as measured by clocks and calendars. On the level of the spirit, some seconds are the equivalent of hours, as some hours are the equivalent of seconds. When we listen to a beautiful symphony, when we are taken up outside ourselves by some beautiful song or by music that totally ravishes us, we are no longer conscious of time passing; in the same way, a person under the stress of fear or horror sometimes imagines that he has been caught up with it for hours whereas it may actually only have been minutes. These considerations provide us with some hint of how difficult it is for us to represent to ourselves accurately what the joy or the pain of souls that have passed on must be like in the state that they are in.

What should we envisage for Purgatory, then, since we seem to need some kind of adequate image in order to sustain faith?

First of all, let us imagine the state of the soul at its entry into the Beyond: it has been liberated from the miseries of this world, it is filled with repentance for sins committed, and it is also carried away by the attraction of approaching God. However, the soul is not yet, for all of that, completely transformed; rather it is like a husband who has lashed out at his wife but who at a word from her, suddenly calms down, throws his arms around her neck and implores her pardon for having been angry at her. There is a quick reconciliation but for how long? The wife will certainly not at one stroke change the behavior of hers that irritated her husband in the first place; nor will his irritability disappear completely at one stroke. A deep conversion requires more time than a superficial reconciliation. New falls, new conflicts can occur owing to the fact that the persons remain imperfect. It will be the same when the soul enters the next world no matter how ardent the soul might be, or how good its intentions, the soul will still not be established in that perfection which alone can make possible its happy communion with God. Except for the rare individual who has achieved in this life a total mystical union with God and through acts of perfect charity has expiated for all his sins, the Church teaches the believer's struggle and purgation of evil continues after death. Those who die in the hope of rising again no longer fear eternal damnation but begin an even more deep cooperation with God's healing grace. The individual does not carry on this cooperation alone but is also assisted by the prayers of the Church on earth and in heaven.

What should we think about the Masses that the Church encourages us to offer for the dead? This is not a superstition; it is the expression of a charity which understands its duty to watch over all who have believed in Jesus and from Him, received His precept of love. It is useless to make as big a thing out of charity as the Church actually does if it avails only for this life. In Jesus Christ, our dead are as present to us as our living brothers; they are even closer since, purified in God, they are even more capable of pure and disinterested love for us. And we can more easily return the same attentive and affectionate sentiments towards them. St. Augustine has explained very well the Church's traditional thought in this matter in the following question:

> It is impossible to deny . . . that the souls of the dead are helped by the prayers of the living, by the sacrifice of the Mass of the One Mediator being offered for them, or by alms distributed in Church for them . . . Of course, these works only help those who, while alive, merited the place where prayers could avail (St. Augustine, *Enchiridion*, 29.109).

But since we do not finally know the ultimate destiny of our dead who have passed into the beyond, it is as natural and normal that we should pray for them as that we should pray for friends on a journey:

> For when the sacrifice of the altar or alms are offered for the dead who have been baptized, they can be considered actions of superabundant grace for those who were in any case entirely good; for those who were not entirely bad, they can be considered a means of propitiation; while for those whose malice was total, and who are beyond help, they are at least a consolation for the living (St. Augustine, *Enchiridion*, 29.110).

The only grave caution that has to be added in considering this matter of the help we render to the dead is that we should never render it at the expense of what we owe to the living. This is all the more the case when we consider the importance St. Augustine places upon "alms distributed in the Church" for the dead: this help to the living is also a help for the souls of the dead. We should never forget that Jesus reproached the Pharisees who, instead of helping their aged parents in their misery, instead offered a *corban* (gift) to the Temple for their own personal salvation. We should never reach the point where the stipends for Masses for the dead transform into such a *"corban"* the goods that we should be offering to our needy brothers and sisters in this world.

7. How do you view Hell then? And why do you prefer the doctrine of Hell to the doctrine of reincarnation?

I don't care to compare two different hells, but I submit that the doctrine of reincarnation actually subjects us to the torture of Sisyphus—which is a kind of perpetual punishment. Sisyphys, the King of Corinth, for his cruelties and brigandages, was condemned to roll a huge stone up the side of a mountain in Hades, from which it would continually roll back down again. Reincarnation, as it was conceived at the time of the principal Upanishads, really came down to pretty much the same thing: it condemned both the good and the bad to a series of continual reincarnations—each of which entailed the possibility of a new fall and, as can easily be imagined, did not entail any promise of a continuous ascension towards the good and the beautiful. Merely a return into another body was no guarantee of returning to live a saintlier life. Assuming that I am living through my 1000th reincarnation, I do not see that I am either far enough advanced in holiness or guaranteed from committing some sin which will drop me back down into another reincarnation worse than my present one.

What is the relationship between God and the damned soul? We do not really know. Jesus clearly gives us to understand that the just inherit eternal life, while the impious receive an eternal punishment (Mt 25:46). If Jesus does not know what He is talking about, then He is not the Son of God and there is no point in paying any attention to anything He says or reposing any confidence whatever in holy Scripture. If, however, Jesus is the Son of God, to Whom the Father has confided the task of judging the world and the living and the dead (Jn 5:27), then He must know what He is talking about. For the rest, I hold, as a personal theological opinion which no one is obliged to agree with, that the damned soul itself refuses the final appeal of the divine mercy at the ultimate moment of choice; the soul refuses to "bet on" God and prefers its own "self-realization." At that point Christ can hardly "condemn" such a soul to live with Him throughout all eternity; to be asked to love someone whose friendship one has already pointedly refused is scarcely a beatitude, but rather a form of torture. Thus God allows those who have refused all of His advances here below to continue to be alienated from Him.[44] To this conclusion we may add that God reserves a different judgment for Christians who have been recipients of His mercy than He does for pagans infinitely excusable for having loved Him less. The category of sin in the normal sense does not apply to infants or severely mentally handicapped people who lack the capacity to either accept or reject Christ freely and with proper understanding. Most theologians today are leaning towards the theory that such individuals at the moment of death are given the opportunity, the special grace, personally to either accept or reject Christ and His freely offered gift of eternal life.

8. Why do you go to such lengths to try to demonstrate that reincarnation is false? Does not the "baptism of desire" suffice to insure salvation for all men regardless of their religion?

It is only too true today that there is a tendency to correct the old dictum, "no salvation outside the Church," with its contrary, which on the lips of some, actually becomes something more like, "salvation everywhere except in the Church!" In this abuse of reason ("thesis and antithesis"), we find something of the ancient "Frankish fury" that made St. Remy cry out at the baptism of Clovis: "Adore now what you formerly burned; burn what you formerly adored!" The proper balance and view of the whole are lacking. If what I have shown about reincarnation is valid—and simply contradicts Christianity—it follows that either one or the other of those who opt for reincarnation or Christianity respectively has to be in error. It is, of course, possible to go on living in error, but not without harm, and, indeed, progressively increasing harm, since one error leads on to additional errors. If truth is the first and greatest good of all men, it is a duty stemming from our obligation to love our neighbor to try to lead others away from error.

I have tried to show, especially in the Conclusion to this work, that the Spirit of God was not entirely absent from the religious history of India. The doctrine of reincarnation originally represented an essential religious truth for men: the realization of their survival. The development of this doctrine made for progress in individual morality and a greater sense of the personal responsibility required of man towards himself; this progress was also a grace of God. The movement that produced the Upanishads, even if it encouraged skepticism and so lost the sense of God's transcendence by its embrace of monism and pantheism, was nevertheless able to destroy a certain cultural-based belief in magic and to combat the sort of Pharisaism that is found to some degree in all religions. The Bhakti movement, finally, by a fortunate return to religious roots arrived at a notion of divine mercy and goodness that is close to Christianity. However, these good elements, elements of *grace*, were incomplete, and, for that reason, sometimes fell into unfortunate deviations. Belief in reincarnation can tempt one to suicide. In calling man to a strict morality, it can give the impression that it is possible to save oneself by one's own *justice*. The skepticism of the Upanishads, finally, led to the divinization of the "I," or self, the worst of all idolatries, in fact. Even the Bhakti movement sometimes fell into eroticism and into types of love of God and neighbor which became a far cry from true charity.

Consequently, even though it is just and honest to recognize the value of the Indian religious experience, it is also just, as well as honest and charitable, to show how Christianity alone brings to completion all these human preparations for an ultimate *truth* that in its totality can only come from God. This is not, of course, a matter for Christian pride but only for recognition of the grave responsibilities that Christians have, once healed from their own deviations, to be the bearers to all men, their brothers, of the truth that will heal them too. It is to us now that the words apply which St. Paul addressed to the Jews of his day: "By boasting about the Law [i.e., for us, the Gospels] and then disobeying it, you bring God into contempt. As Scripture says: It is your fault that the name of God is blasphemed among the pagans" (Rm 2:33).

Another verse of St. Paul's also applies to us: "Not that I boast of preaching the Gospel, since it is a duty that has been laid upon me; I should be punished if I did not preach it!" (1 Cor 9:16).

Jesus did not command His disciples to go and be evangelized by all the nations; on the contrary, He commanded them: "Go . . . make disciples of all nations, baptizing them . . . and teaching them to observe all the commands I gave you" (Mt 28:19). I wouldn't go to so much trouble to recall all this if I were not so aware of how far a taste for ill-digested ecumenism has carried so many Christians—not in order to help unbelievers come to the truth but rather nudge believers onto a path that leads towards the rejection of the Gospels. The true apostolic path enjoins upon us to "live by the truth and in love" (Ep 4:15) and not to sacrifice truth under the pretext of practicing charity; the latter can, in fact, be nothing else but a false love of neighbor leading us to compromise with error and with the things that enslave and prevent one from true and full self-realization.

9. *Why not strike an alliance with Yoga?*

We first have to distinguish between authentic Indian Yoga, which arose out of a particular combination of magic and religion, and occidental Yoga, habitually pursued as a method of relaxation or meditation or a means to approach the divine.

In the case of authentic Indian Yoga, as it was taken up and adapted by the movement which produced the Upanishads and developed up to the present day, it promises an escape from the endless cycle of births and entry into nirvana. It thus claims to be a veritable means of *salvation*—at least for those who believe in reincarnation and fear it. But this salvation is not acquired for nothing: it assumes a belief in the doctrine of the identity of the Self with God, and, for us Christians, that doctrine is unacceptable from every point of view: 1) we cannot accept that there is any sense in which God is merged with the creature, and hence that there *can* be any "identity" between the personal self and God; 2) we cannot accept that there is any sense in which man *saves himself*, that is, without reference to the redemptive death and the resurrection of our Savior (Whom no adept of an Indian Gnosticism can ever accept from his own point of view); nor 3) can we accept in any sense that, at the end of its earthly pilgrimage, the human soul is somehow *dissolved* back into the Creator viewed as some kind of impersonal universal principle. As a consequence of these clear points, there is nothing for the Christian in the idea that his goal is a nirvana which can be sought in the course of this life by means of Yoga or transcendental meditation. To profess or teach such a belief, in fact, is to fall into the most melancholy of errors and, indeed, simply to reject the most fundamental doctrines of Christianity.

Even to teach Yoga as a method of relaxation, whether it is Mantra Yoga or any other type, is, I contend, also a proceeding requiring a great deal of prudence. Yoga is actually a kind of *drug*, and it is as such that it is taught in a number of American schools— as a supposedly inoffensive substitute for LSD and other hallucinatory substances. In fact, it is a drug that is always available to anyone at any time, once its techniques have been mastered; one can quickly become an addict of it. For it is a drug of uncontested efficaciousness whose effects can be powerful though little understood. In the state of enstasy that it brings, the subject's subconscious is given free rein precisely because the reason is made dormant. It is not surprising that under these circumstances numerous adepts of transcendental meditation, in particular the professors of this kind of meditation, have occasionally given themselves over to suicide or to other reprehensible acts; there remained nothing in them to resist their suicidal tendencies, their will to power, or their desires for vengeance. Rabindranath R. Muharaj, in his book *Death of a Guru*, tells us how he wanted to kill his aunt who had accused him of being a "good-for-nothing" like his father in practicing transcendental meditation. Why would such an author attempt to deceive us in a matter that reflected so little honor on himself? I have heard persons who practiced transcendental meditation admit that they simply became dominated by their mantra; this is what finally frightened Maharaj and induced him to give up this method of so-called relaxation which had become the source of terrible obsessions for him.

Finally, if it is proposed that Yoga should be transformed into a method of Christian prayer, then I must clearly state, as far as I am concerned, that the risk of confusion here is very great and so are the dangers. If God is confused with the "I" or the unconscious mind, self-absorption could be interpreted as an ascent towards God; for us Christians that would be an aberrant view. God is in fact the Wholly Other and it is *outside ourselves* that we must seek for Him.[45] There are, of course, different methods of prayer and contemplation in Christianity; and fasts, silences and concentration can prepare for them. But all these things are a far cry from Yoga. If all that Yoga did was to help in relaxation or concentration, it could be as useful as any other method in accomplishing these desired aims. But Yoga goes far beyond this: it gives one over to the unconscious mind, to visions and interior journeys and to all the possible deviations that might arise from these. Yoga can even help some subjects develop undeniable "powers" over the material world which can then serve as temptations for them rather than as invitations to renounce the world in favor of God.

We must recognize, of course, that the great Christian mystics have gone through periods of ecstasy and rapture. But I emphasize the interpretation that they themselves have generally placed upon such experiences: they regarded them as signs of the weakness of their condition at the beginning of their spiritual life, at a time when they were not yet able to sustain the shock of experiencing the divine. Another thing is certain: Jesus never made ecstasy a condition of entering into His kingdom. Furthermore, when the Church canonizes a saint, whether it is a St. Teresa of Avila or a St. John of the Cross, no consideration is accorded to their visions or raptures, but only to their conduct, to a moral life of theirs characterized by faith, hope, and charity and capable of serving as a model for a Christian people.

I do not say any of this in order to condemn mysticism—which has had such a bad press in the Church since the Jansenism of Pierre Nicole and the controversies over Quietism. I even believe that mysticism in a certain sense is more important to the Church than morality if the latter is understood merely as servile observance without any love of the law of the Gospel. But I do not for all of that identify "mysticism" with "mystical-type phenomena," the latter of which can sometimes be all too natural and capable of being exhaustively explained by psychology or parapsychology. But I still retain my admiration of the great Indian spiritual man who sought God by means of different methods of Yoga; it was their *quest for God* that was admirable.

We have also seen Christians who have passed their lives living on top of columns or inflicting various and severe punishments on themselves (one such as Henri Suso, for example, to whom Jesus Himself had to appear to forbid such extreme practices); but the fact that such extreme disciples have been encountered among Christians does not necessarily mean that they are all equally *evangelical* and free of danger. "Spiritual combat is as brutal as human battle, but the vision of justice is God's pleasure alone." Let us not confuse our justice with that of God, nor the methods by which we pursue that justice with the divine justice of the kingdom which is "our wisdom, and our virtue, and our holiness, and our freedom" (1 Cor 1:30).

10. How do we distinguish between reincarnation and resurrection?

Reincarnation, as the idea is encountered in Indian or African religions, or in modern Gnosticisms, holds to a belief in the passing of a dead person's soul into *another body* than its own original body, whether this body is human, animal, vegetable or mineral.

Resurrection, as it is encountered in the Bible, takes two forms:

a. Temporal Resurrection. In this category, we find the cases of the son of the Shunammite raised up by Elijah (2 K 4:8ff.); of the daughter of Jairus raised by Jesus (Lk 8:54); of the son of the widow of Nain raised by Him (Lk 7:11); and of Lazarus (Jn 11:1ff.). To these cases, we may add the cases of Enoch and Elijah from the Jewish tradition that was not received by the Church; it was believed that they would return at the end of the world. None of these are cases of incarnation, of course, since no souls pass into other bodies; the original bodies are simply resuscitated.

b. Final Resurrection. The Christian faith teaches that, at the end of the world, all human souls will take up again the bodies that were their companions during their earthly existence. The souls of the just will have glorified bodies transformed in the same way as that of Jesus Christ (Ph 3:21); the souls of unregenerate sinners will have miserable bodies condemned to "eternal punishment"

(Mt 25:46). Here, again, we are not talking about reincarnation because: 1) the soul is not passing into another body but is rather taking up again its own original body reconstituted by the power of God; and 2) this transformation is effected only once, indeed "once for all," since there can be no question of any cycle of births in Christianity.

11. Is reincarnation an absolute impossibility then?

If one admits the existence of a creator God and His providence, as is the case with the ancient Indian and African religions, reincarnation is not an absolute impossibility. Thus, as it has been imagined in African religion, a merciful God could permit a soul already transported to the "village of ancestors" to redescend to earth and take up a new abode in a woman's womb in order to help a family or clan that had prayed for that soul's return. This might indeed be possible. What we Christians affirm on this point, though, is that God has nowhere revealed to us that He might or would act in this fashion; and it is the revelation that we in fact have in Jesus Christ that is our unique rule of faith in these matters.

If, however, one conceives of God as a blind force, as cosmic energy, or as an impersonal being—and these are, in fact, the conceptions of God that dominate both the Upanishads and the most typical Gnosticisms—then there is a serious question about why a soul would choose to be reincarnated back into another body. If one *is* impersonal, it is idle to speak of choice, in fact; one has neither choice nor preference. Also, how is it possible to conceive of a "law" of Karma without postulating the existence of a lawgiver? All law presupposes an intelligence laying it down. This is why consistent atheists do not habitually speak of order or pattern in the world but instead see chance, accident and absurdity everywhere. But to see these things and *also* to go on speaking about reincarnation is to fall into gross contradiction and even incoherence. It is for the Gnosticisms that, given their overall viewpoint, reincarnation ought to be an impossibility; yet they are the very ones who preach reincarnation!

Footnotes

44. We must not forget what I wrote on this point in Part Two, Chapter V, about the "second death" and the "lake of fire."
45. The musician who closes his eyes to appreciate more fully the quality of the sound does not, for all of that, have a tuning fork in his belly. Similarly the great Christian mystics who invite their human brothers to look inside themselves in order to find God more easily do not mean by that that God is somehow "more" really present in the human heart than elsewhere. It is important to distinguish between "a manner of speaking," and what is being expressed.

CHRISTIAN TEACHINGS ABOUT
THE HUMAN SOUL

I have collected here some of the official traditional teachings of the Church concerning some of the questions which have concerned us up to now. These texts are far from having the greatest dogmatic value; it is surprising how little concern there has been in official Church teachings for some of these questions:

I. The human soul is not an integral part and parcel of God as the Gnostics have believed.

"If anyone shall say and believe that the human soul is a portion of God, or that it is the substance of God, let him be anathema" (Council of Toledo, A.D. 400-447).

"If anyone shall believe that human souls or angels are part of the substance of God, as Mani and Priscillian have said, let him be anathema" (Council of Braga, A.D. 563).

"There is in the soul something that is uncreated and uncreatable; if the entire soul were it, the soul too would be uncreated and uncreatable—it is the intellect"[46] (Condemned Proposition, among the Condemnation of the Errors of Eckhart, March 27, 1329).

II. The human soul did not preexist the human body.

"If anyone shall say or think that the souls of men preexist, in this sense that they were previously spirits or spiritual powers that, growing tired of the contemplation of God, they turned towards an inferior state; or that, for this reason, the charity of God grew cold in them, which was what caused them to be called 'souls' in Greek (*psyche*), and that they were sent to inhabit bodies as a punishment—let him be anathema" (Synod of Constantinople, A.D. 543).[47]

"If anyone shall say that human souls sinned in heavenly places and that it is for that reason that they have come down to earth in bodies, as Priscillian has held, let him be anathema" (Council of Braga, A.D. 563).[48]

III. The human soul is by itself the substantial form of the human body and is not merely accidentally allied to it.[49]

"We reprove as erroneous and opposed to the Catholic faith every doctrine or thesis temerariously affirming that the substance of the rational and intellectual soul is not truly and by itself the form of the human body or casting doubt upon this; and we define, in order that all might know the true faith and that the door might be closed to the surreptitious entry of all error that whoever might dare henceforth to affirm that the rational and intellectual soul is not of itself and essentially the form of the body has to be considered a heretic" (Council of Vienne, 15th Ecumenical Council, 1311-12).

"We condemn and reprove with the sanction of this holy synod, all those who affirm that the intellectual soul is mortal or unique in all men and all those who have doubts about this question, because not only is the soul truly and of itself essentially the form of the human body, according to the sense of the canon which Pope Clement V of happy memory gave to the Council of Vienne [i.e., the preceding text], but it is also immortal, and, in view of the multitude of bodies in which souls are infused, it can be multiplied, is multiplied, and must be multiplied individually" (5th Lateran Council, 18th ecumenical council, 1513).[50]

"We know that these same books [of Dr. Anton Gunther] offend Catholic thought and the doctrine that man is composed of a body and a soul in such a manner that the rational soul is itself and truly the immediate form of the body" (Brief of Pope Pius IX to Cardinal Geissel, dated June 15, 1857).

"The opinion which situates in man a unique life principle, that is, the rational soul, from which the body itself takes its movements, the totality of its life and its sensations, is the most common opinion in the Church of God; it has appeared to the majority of thinkers and doctors as linked with the highest dogmas of the faith and as the one true interpretation, and it is impossible to deny it without danger to faith."[51]

Footnotes

46. The condemnation of this proposition by the Church is of capital importance, for it is on this very point that the false mystics of India take their stand. Master Eckhart is seen to be classic Gnostic on this point. It is not surprising that modern Gnostics claim him as one of their own.
47. This is a condemnation of the doctrine of Origen, which is not exactly the same as Platonic reincarnation.
48. This is a condemnation of a doctrine similar to Origen's, a doctrine which is for the most part identical to Indian conceptions.
49. This proposition implies the rejection of the very possibility of reincarnation, since the same and single principle cannot inform two composites.
50. The doctrine condemned here is not reincarnation as such but Gnosticism which imagines that there is only a single, impersonal spirit (the "Self") present in all human beings.
51. We have to recognize the obstacle which prevented the Councils, from the Middle Ages on, from simply declaring, plainly and clearly, that the soul was the "substantial form" of the body; this obstacle was the fact that Thomist and Bonaventurist theologians were disagreed on this particular point. To avoid pointless conflicts and disputes on a matter that is philosophical rather than that of the faith as such—and on which the Scriptures are silent—the Catholic Church has preferred to eliminate specific errors about the soul as they arose rather than setting forth a comprehensive doctrine about the nature of the soul and the relationship of the soul to the body.

APPENDIX

TEXTS CONCERNING THE

DOCTRINE OF REINCARNATION

AND THE RESURRECTION

I

THE ORIGIN OF REINCARNATION
ACCORDING TO PLATO

The Demiurge created as many souls as there are stars, and then laid down the laws by which their destinies would be governed:

"At the first birth the condition of all souls will be equal so that there will be no disadvantaged among them; entering into Time and distributed throughout the universe,[1] these souls will take on the nature most capable of honoring the gods.[2]

"However, human nature being dual, superiority must be deemed to reside in the *virile* sex.[3] Once souls have been implanted in bodies, and the person's actions have resulted in either losses or gains[4] . . . he who has lived right will mount towards the particular star assigned to him to dwell there in a condition of happiness that conforms to the state of his soul.[5] However, he who has failed the test will be reborn again, changing his nature for that of a woman.[6]

"If, in this new nature, the soul does not cease and desist from its malice, it will be reincarnated continuously into animal bodies according to the nature of its vice.[7] Through such continued metamorphoses, it will never see the end of the penalties it must suffer."[8]

Having made known to souls these dispositions of the laws by which their destinies would be governed—definitely not foreknowing the malice to which any of them might become prey[9]— the Demiurge then thrust the created souls into Time, distributing them throughout the earth and moon.

PLATO, *Timaeus*

Footnotes

1. For example, on the moon which, in antiquity, served as the measure of both months and years, and was held to be inhabited along with the earth and the other planets.
2. That is, human nature; these souls will animate an intelligent human being, alone among creatures able to believe in the gods and raise up altars for their worship.
3. All human beings were supposedly made at the outset; reincarnation in a woman's body was held to be the result of a *fall*. In contrast, according to the Bible, God Himself created woman to be man's companion and helpmate (and equal): ". . . bone from my bone, and flesh from my flesh" (Gn 2:22).
4. Plato is saying, in a passage that is far from clear, that men thus implanted in bodies will necessarily have passions (desire, anger, fear, etc.), but that some men will dominate these passions while others will be dominated by them; the reincarnation of the latter types of men in inferior bodies will constitute their punishment.
5. This concept of Plato's is similar to that of the Aryan religion in which those who have lived right will inhabit a blessed realm on the moon—for the ancients, another star.
6. In Greece, as in India, to be born a woman is the consequence of a fault committed in a previous existence.
7. Plato elsewhere describes the effects of these unhappy reincarnations, i.e., in *Phaedo*: "Those for whom gluttony, excess and passion for drink have been regularly indulged without any effort being exerted to master these vices will no doubt see their souls implanted in the bodies of donkeys or similar beasts."
8. That is, until the soul learns to govern the passions of the body which it inhabits and to practice virtue.
9. Since men so easily and naturally blame the Deity for their unhappy state, Plato intends here to explain that they have only themselves to blame for that state, and, if they find themselves incarnated in miserable bodies, it is because of their conduct in a previous existence.

II

DANGERS OF A SOUL'S SELF-KNOWLEDGE
NOT ACCOMPANIED BY
A COMPARABLE KNOWLEDGE OF GOD

During the time of ancient ignorance, that is to say, during the time that preceded the advent of Jesus Christ, the human soul's knowledge of its own dignity and immortality as often as not led it astray.

The cult of the dead was one of the constant characteristics of idolatry; almost all pagans sacrificed to the shades, that is, to the souls of the dead. Contemplating these ancient superstitions, we can see how ancient is the belief in the immortality of the soul; this belief must constitute one of the oldest traditions of the human race.

Man, who naturally botches everything anyway, certainly did not draw the correct conclusions from his belief in immortality, since he was only induced by it to sacrifice to the souls of the dead. Primitive man even went to the point of human sacrifice: his slaves and even his women were slaughtered in order to enable their souls to serve the dead in another world. Like many other peoples, the ancient Gauls had such practices. The Indians, notable among pagan peoples for their defense of the doctrine of the immortality of the soul, also introduced, on the pretext of religion, these abominable sacrificial murders.

The Indians also killed themselves in order to advance their happiness in a future life, and this deplorable error still persists among them. We thus see how dangerous it can be to teach even truths—apart from the order and context established by God—or to try to explain these truths to man before he has first understood Who God is.

It was because they did not truly know God that a majority of the philosophers who believed in the immortality of the soul also believed that that same soul was a portion of the divinity itself, an eternal entity, uncreated as well as incorruptible, with neither beginning nor end.

What can I really say about those who believed in the transmigration of souls? Who indeed would have thus moved souls from heaven down to earth and back to heaven again, from animals into men and from men into animals, from happiness to misery and from misery back to happiness, without any term ever being set as to how long the whole process would continue to go on?

In the midst of such errors, there was little wonder that God's Providence, His justice and His goodness all became obscured. It is clear how strictly necessary it was to know God and the authentic laws established by His wisdom before one could properly appreciate the truth that the soul is immortal.

JACQUES-BENIGNE BOSSUET,
Discourse on Universal History,
1681, Part II, Chapter XIX

III

ACHIEVING ENSTASY BY DRINKING SOMA

Drink raises me up
Like a furious wind.[1]
Did I drink soma?

Drink pulls me up
Like a swift team of horses drawing a chariot.
Did I drink soma?

Divine thoughts come to me
The way the cow lows towards her beloved calf.
Did I drink soma?

As a carpenter fashions a chariot-seat,
So I fashion the prayer of my soul.
Did I drink soma?

The five different races of men
Are not worth the blink of any eye.
Did I drink soma?

As a whole the two great worlds
Do not amount to more than I do by myself.
Did I drink soma?

I will fix the place
of the earth itself, here or there.
Did I drink soma?

I will strike the earth thus fixed,
Here or there, to destroy it.
Did I drink soma?

I stand with one foot in heaven already,
The other on earth.
Did I drink soma?

I am great, great,[2]
See how I am carried up to the clouds!
Did I drink soma?

I am a well-furnished house that walks,
A sacrificial fire offered to the gods.
Did I drink soma?

RIG VEDA 9.119, Marabout University,
No. 145, pp. 78-9

Footnotes

1. The singer demands from soma, a brown-colored juice brewed from a plant,
   the same result that others would later demand from Yoga and transcendental
   meditation, namely, a state of *enstasy* beyond consciousness in which the
   subject acquires mysterious knowledge and approaches God more closely.
2. We get the impression that soma produces all the hallucinations characteristic
   of LSD: feelings of greatness and strength and release from a subconscious
   more and more ready to explode with dangerous consequences both for the
   individual involved and for anyone around him in case of such an explosion.

IV

SLEEP AND DREAMS

Which is the soul?
The person here who is made of knowledge, who is the light in the heart. He, remaining the same, goes along both worlds, appearing to think, appearing to move about, for upon becoming asleep he transcends this world and the forms of death.

Verily, this person, by being born and obtaining a body, is joined with evils. When he departs, on dying, he leaves evils behind.

Verily, there are just two conditions of this person: the condition of being in this world and the condition of being in the other world. There is an intermediate third condition, namely, that of being in sleep. By standing in this intermediate condition, one sees both those conditions, namely, being in this world and being in the other world, by making that approach one sees the evils [of this world] and the joys [of yonder world].

When one goes to sleep, he takes along the material of this all-containing world, himself tears it apart, himself builds it up, and dreams by his own brightness, by his own light. Then this person becomes self-illuminated.

There are no chariots there, no spans, no roads. But he projects from himself chariots, spans, roads. There are no blisses there, no pleasures, no delights. But he projects from himself blisses, pleasures and delights. There are no tanks there, no lotus-pools, no streams. But he projects from himself tanks, lotus-pools, streams. For he is a creator.[1]

BRIHAD-ARANYAKA UPANISHAD 4.3 7-10[2]

Footnotes

1. We must not, however, make the mistake of believing that for the Upanishads, this world amounts to anything. On the contrary, it is nothing but illusion and deception. What the sage must seek, as the Hindu theologian Shankara made clear, is a sleep *without* dreams, a plunge into total unconsciousness, prefiguring nirvana.

2. From *The Thirteen Principal Upanishads*, Translated from the Sanscrit with an Outline of the Philosophy of the Upanishads, by Robert Ernest Hume, Second Edition, Revised (paperback), Oxford University Press, London, 1971, p. 134.

V

THE HOW OF REINCARNATION ACCORDING TO THE INDIAN CONCEPTION

Those who in the village reverence a belief in sacrifice, merit, and almsgiving—they pass into the smoke [of the funeral pyre];[1] from the smoke, into the night; from the night, into the latter half of the month; from the latter half of the month, into the six months during which the sun moves southward—these do not reach the year; from those months, into the world of the fathers; from the world of the fathers, into space; from space, into the moon. That is King Soma. That is the food of the gods. The gods eat that.[2]

After having remained in it as long as there is a residue [of their good works],[3] then by that course by which they came they return again, just as they came, into space; from space, into wind. After having become wind, one becomes smoke. After having become smoke, he becomes mist.

After having become mist, he becomes cloud. After having become cloud, he rains down.[4] They are born here as rice and barley, as herbs and trees, as sesame plants and beans. Thence, verily, indeed, it is difficult to emerge; for only if someone or other eats him as food and emits him as semen, does he develop further.[5]

Accordingly, those who are of pleasant conduct here—the prospect is indeed that they will enter a pleasant womb, either the womb of Brahman, or the womb of a Kshatriya, or the womb of a

Vaisya. But those who are of stinking conduct here—the prospect is, indeed, that they will enter a stinking womb, either the womb of a dog, or the womb of a swine, or the womb of an outcast (*candala*).[6]

CHANDOGYA UPANISHAD 5.10.3-7[7]

Footnotes

1. This refers to the journey of the soul which begins when the body is placed on the funeral pyre: the soul escapes with the smoke, enveloped in its "subtle body."
2. Literally: King Soma *devours* the soul. It is hard to see how this conception is intended to describe a *happy* future life among the gods.
3. It is necessary that there remain a residue of the soul's good works in its "subtle body" because this residue is the *seed* of its subsequent reincarnation.
4. The slipping into the singular here, from "they" to "it," indicates a reworking and editing of this text. The idea that souls make use of raindrops to return to earth is a belief found among various peoples.
5. It is impossible to understand how a soul with good works to its credit could possibly be reincarnated thus in plants; elsewhere such a reincarnation is considered the worst of punishments, since the means of expiation and passage into a more fruitful reincarnation becomes almost impossible.
6. The harshness of the vision depicted here bears witness, in my opinion, to the author's skepticism about any reincarnation in the real sense: he makes it appear as inexorable as possible in order to win over the reader to his view of Gnosticism as the only way to escape the painful prospects inherent in reincarnation.
7. From Hume, *op. cit.*, Appendix IV, p. 233.

VI

LIBERATION BY MEANS OF GNOSTICISM

The sages who, adoring being, become shorn of all desire, pass beyond reincarnation.[1]

He who, in his mind, continues desiring desire, is condemned to rebirth by this very desire.[2] But for him whose Atman [the divine self in each person] is fulfilled and his desires granted, all desire here below becomes extinct.

Now this Atman cannot be apprehended by means of doctrines, or of sacrifices, or of arduous study.[3] Only he apprehends it who wills to do so; it is this Atman that reveals its own nature. . . .[4]

This Atman cannot be apprehended by a man who lacks the strength, nor by means of an inadequate asceticism. But he who makes the effort to apprehend it by these means [transcendental meditation, asceticism], if he is truly wise, his Atman will enter into the sphere of Brahman. . . .

Those ascetics who have the specific goal of acquiring the knowledge of the Vedanta, and who resolve upon a course of complete renunciation—it is they who are pure and, raised to the sphere of Brahman, will surmount death at the supreme moment and achieve deliverance. . . .

Just as rivers flow into the sea and are absorbed and lost there, losing their individual names and forms, so it will be for the one who *knows*; he will be freed from his name and form [identity], becoming merged with the divine, more exalted than one can even imagine.[5]

He who knows the supreme Brahman thus becomes this Brahman. No one of this type can be any longer ignorant of Brahman. He passes beyond suffering. He passes beyond evil. Delivered from interior constraints, he becomes immortal.

MUNDAKA UPANISHAD, III.2.1,
Marabout University, No. 146

Footnotes

1. They slough off the soul's "subtle body," which bears the seeds of reincarnation.
2. This comes very close to the key idea of Buddhism: the extinction of all desire.
3. This assertion amounts to a rejection of the original Vedic religion and of its theology.
4. The "I" becoming conscious of its own divinity, in other words.
5. In this kind of concept we see the beginnings of the evolutionist's illusion that the world is "a machine to produce gods."

VII-A

JONATHAN LIVINGSTON SEAGULL: THE INDIAN DOCTRINE OF REINCARNATION IN AN OCCIDENTAL CONTEXT

It happened just a week later. Fletcher was demonstrating the elements of high-speed flying to a class of new students. He had just pulled out of his dive from seven thousand feet, a long gray streak firing a few inches above the beach, when a young bird on its first flight glided directly into his path, calling for its mother. With a tenth of a second to avoid the youngster, Fletcher Lynd Seagull snapped hard to the left at something over two hundred miles per hour, into a cliff of solid granite.

It was, for him, as though the rock were a giant hard door into another world. A burst of fear and shock and black as he hit, and then he was adrift in a strange sky, forgetting, remembering, forgetting; afraid and sad and sorry, terribly sorry.

The voice came to him as it had in the first day that he had met Jonathan Livingston Seagull.

"The trick, Fletcher, is that we are trying to overcome our limitations in order, patiently. We don't tackle flying through rock until a little later in the program."

"Jonathan!"

"Also known as the Son of the Great Gull," the instructor said dryly.

"What are you doing here? The cliff! Haven't I . . . didn't I . . . die?"

"Oh, Fletch, come on. Think. If you are talking to me now, then obviously you didn't die, did you? What you did manage to do was to change your level of consciousness rather abruptly. It's your choice now. You can stay here and learn on this level—which is quite a bit higher than the one you left, by the way—or you can go back and keep working with the Flock. The Elders were hoping for some kind of disaster, but they're startled that you obliged them so well."

"I want to go back to the Flock, of course. I've barely begun with the new group!"

"Very well, Fletcher. Remember what we were saying about one's body being nothing more than thought itself . . .?"

Fletcher shook his head and stretched his wings and opened his eyes at the base of the cliff, in the center of the whole Flock assembled. There was a great clamor of squawks and screes from the crowd when first he moved.

"He lives! He that was dead lives!"

RICHARD BACH, *Jonathan Livingston Seagull: A Story*, Avon Books, New York, 1973, pp. 116-121.[1]

Footnotes

1. It has to be mentioned that young people have actually committed suicide on the strength of this particular passage. The doctrine of reincarnation can motivate this among those who do not realize that God exists and that He might punish those who take it upon themselves to dispose of their lives which in fact they hold in stewardship from God.

VII-B

THE GOD OF THE PHILOSOPHERS
AND SAVANTS

When I am told, then, by the partisans of Universities without Theological teaching, that human science leads to belief in a Supreme Being, without denying the fact, nay, as a Catholic, with full conviction of it, nevertheless I am obliged to ask what the statement means in *their* mouths, what they, the speakers, understand by the word "God." Let me not be thought offensive, if I question, whether it means the same thing on the two sides of the controversy.

With us Catholics . . . God is an Individual, Self-dependent, All-perfect, Unchangeable Being; intelligent, living, personal, and present; almighty, all-seeing, all-remembering; between whom and His creatures there is an infinite gulf; who has no origin, who is all-sufficient for Himself; who created and upholds the universe; who will judge every one of us, sooner or later, according to that Law of right and wrong which He has written on our heart. He is One who is sovereign over, operative amidst, independent of, the appointments which He has made; One in whose hands are all things, who has a purpose in every event, and a standard for every deed. . . .

This is the doctrine which belief in a God implies in the mind of a Catholic: if it means anything, it means all this, and cannot keep from meaning all this, and a great deal more; and, even though there were nothing in the religious tenets of the last three centuries to disparage dogmatic truth, still, even then, I should have difficulty in believing that a doctrine so mysterious, so peremptory, approved itself as a matter of course to educated men of this day, who gave their minds attentively to consider it. Rather, in a state of society such as ours, in which authority, prescription, tradition, habit, moral instinct, and the divine influences go for nothing, in which patience of thought, and depth of consistency of view are scorned as subtle and scholastic, in which free discussion and fallible judgment are prized as the birthright of each individual, I must be excused if I exercise towards this age, as regards its belief in this doctrine, some portion of that skepticism which it exercises towards every received but unscrutinized assertion whatever. I cannot take it for granted, I must have it brought home to me by tangible evidence, that the spirit of age means by the Supreme Being what Catholics mean. Nay, it would be a relief to my mind to gain some ground of assurance, that the parties influenced by that spirit had, I will not say, a true apprehension of God, but even so much as the idea of what a true apprehension is.

Nothing is easier than to use the word, and mean nothing by it. The heathens used to say, "God wills," when they meant "Fate;" "God provides" when they meant "Chance;" "God acts" when they meant "Instinct" or "Sense;" and "God is everywhere," when they meant "the Soul of Nature." The Almighty is something infinitely different from a principle, or a center of action, or a quality, or a generalization of phenomena. If, then, by the word, you do but mean a Being who keeps the world in order, who acts in it, but only in the way of general Providence, who acts towards us but only through what are called laws of Nature, who is more certain not to act at all than to act independently of those laws, who is known and approached indeed, but only through the medium of those laws; such a God is not difficult for anyone to conceive, not difficult for anyone to endure. If, I say, as you would revolutionize heaven, if you have changed the divine sovereignty into a sort of constitutional monarchy, in which the Throne has honor and ceremonial enough, but cannot issue the most ordinary command except through legal forms and precedents, and with the countersignature of a minister, then belief in a God is no more than an acknowledgement of existing, sensible powers and phenomena, which none but an idiot can deny.[1]

> JOHN HENRY CARDINAL NEWMAN, *The Idea of a University*, Edited, with an Introduction and Notes, by Marin J. Svaglic, Holt, Rinehart and Winston, New York, 1960, pp. 27-28.

Footnotes

1. This passage of Newman's is especially significant for those who do not realize that the conception of God that is common to Gnosticism and reincarnational beliefs is usually as materialistic as it is erroneous.

❧

VIII

THE FUTILE HOPE OF REINCARNATION

"How is it possible," the old man[1] asked, "that the philosophers can have the correct views and teach us about God when they themselves know nothing about Him—Whom they have neither seen nor heard?"

"But, father," I replied, "it is not with one's eyes that it is possible to see the divine as one sees other living things. A view of the divine is accorded only to the eyes of our spirit, as Plato says, and I believe it."

"Our spirit is then of such a nature, and strong enough, so that we can perceive being in other ways than through the senses? Can our spirit indeed see God in any other way except if it is granted by the Holy Spirit? Would our spirit be a part of the universal Spirit?"[2]

"Certainly," I declared.

"But are all souls, in all living beings, thus capable of knowing God?" he rejoined. "Or does the human soul differ from that of a horse or a donkey?"[3]

"No, they are the same," I said.

"Horses and donkeys have seen or will see God then?"

"No," I replied. "They will no more see Him than the majority of men will see Him. Only those who live right, purified by justice and the other virtues will see Him . . . While it subsists in human form, the soul can acquire a vision [of God] through our spirit, but the soul will attain to its desires especially when it is discovered when it is delivered from the body, recovering its natural state."

"Does a soul remember a heavenly existence when it comes back into a man?"

"I don't think so."

"What profit is there then for the soul that has seen God over the soul that has not, if there is no memory of it? If it doesn't even remember that it *has* seen?"[4]

ST. JUSTIN, *Dialogue with Trypho*, III and IV.

Footnotes

1. The "old man" in this excerpt speaks as a Christian affirming that only grace, a gift of the Holy Spirit, enables one to "see" God.
2. That is, would the soul itself be divine, a part of the Logos?
3. Those who believed in a reincarnation extending to lower beings, animal or vegetable, had to maintain that all "souls" were equal, or, rather, "human," since other beings were nothing else but reincarnated humans.
4. We will return later on to this same difficulty: what is the point of reincarnation if the reincarnated have no memory of their previous existences? How then can they repent and amend their lives?

IX

DIVINE PROVIDENCE DOES NOT ENTIRELY EXCLUDE EVIL FROM THINGS

The divine government whereby God works among things does not exclude the operation of second causes . . . Now, a defect may occur in an effect through a defect in the secondary active cause, without there being any defect in the first agent. Thus, there may be a defect in the work of a craftsman, who is perfect in his craft, because of some defect in the instrument; even so, a man with healthy locomotive power may limp, through no fault in the locomotive power, but because his leg is not straight. Accordingly, in the things moved and governed by God, defect and evil may be found because of defects in the secondary agents, even though there is no defect in God Himself.

Moreover, perfect goodness would not be found in things unless there were degrees of goodness, so that, namely, there be some things better than others; or else all the possible degrees of goodness would not be fulfilled, nor would any creature be found like to God in the point of being better than others. Moreover, this would do away with the chief beauty in things if the order resulting from distinction and disparity were abolished; and, what is more, the absence of inequality in goodness would involve the elimination of multitude, since it is because things differ from one another that one is better than another: e.g., the animate than the inanimate, and the rational than the irrational. Consequently, if there were absolute equality among things, there would be but one created good; which is clearly derogatory to the goodness of the creature. . . .

Therefore, it does not belong to the divine Providence to remove evil entirely from things. . . .

Hereby is refuted the error of those who, through observing the presence of evil in the world, said that there is no God. Thus Boethius introduces a philosopher who asks: *If there be a God, whence comes evil?* On the contrary, he should have argued: *If there is evil, there is a God.* For there would be no evil if the order of good were removed, the privation of which is evil; and there would be no such order, if there were no God. . . .

ST. THOMAS AQUINAS, *Summa contra Gentiles*,
in *Basic Writings of St. Thomas Aquinas*,
Edited by Anton C. Pegis, Random House,
New York, Vol. II, 1945, pp. 130-32.

X

A RELIGION OF THE INTELLIGENCE

In the beginning, Atman (Self, Soul), verily, one only, was here—no other winking thing whatever. He bethought himself: "Let me now create worlds."[1]

. . . Who is this one? We worship him as the Self (Atman). Which one is the Self? [He] whereby one sees, or whereby one hears, or whereby one smells odors, or whereby one articulates speech, or whereby one discriminates the sweet and the unsweet; that which is heart and mind—that is, consciousness, perception, discrimination, intelligence, wisdom, insight, steadfastness, thought, thoughtfulness, impulse, memory, conception, purpose, life, desire and will.

All these, indeed, are appellations of intelligence.

He is Brahma; he is Indra; he is Prajapati:[2] all these gods; and these five gross elements, namely earth, wind, space, water, light; these things and those which are mingled of the fine, as it were; origins of one sort and another: those born from an egg and those born from a womb, and those born from sweat, and those born from a sprout; horses, cows, persons, elephants; whatever breathing thing there is here—whether moving or flying, and what is stationary.

All this is guided by intelligence, is based on intelligence. The world is guided by intelligence. The basis is intelligence. Brahma is intelligence.[3]

AITAREYA UPANISHAD I.1.1.—III.5.1[4]

Footnotes

1. This author applies to the individual "I" or self the attributes traditionally accorded in Indian religion to Indra, the god-principle of all life.
2. "Prajapati" is a personification (?), or, rather, an abstraction for creative power. This power, wrested from Indra, is transformed here into a kind of vague cosmic energy that animates all living things.
3. Thus the cult of self is substituted for the worship of a personal God. Everything is identified with God and God with everything. There is more than a symbol in the picture of a Yogi trying to approach God by contemplating his *navel*; there is the expression of a sad truth here. The God of Christians is as distant from the intelligence of man as He is from man's body and from the material world; this God is a Beyond, a Wholly Other; He is transcendent.
4. From Hume, *op. cit.*, Appendix IV, pp. 294; 300-01.

XI

INFINITE DIMENSIONS
OF THE PASSION OF CHRIST

It will be clearly seen, following what we have already written, that there is nothing unseemly in confessing that the Son of God suffered and died. We do not attribute these actions to His divine nature, but to that human nature of His that He assumed for the sake of our salvation.

If anyone objects that God, since He is omnipotent, could have saved the human race otherwise than by requiring the death of His only Son, we reply that, where divine actions are concerned, it is necessary to consider whether what has been done is seemly or fitting and not only whether God could have acted otherwise. Whoever considers the second question could as easily object to all the other works of God.

Whoever asks why God made the sky in the dimensions that He did, or why He created the number of stars that He did, if he is wise, will realize that what has been made is good even though it could have been made otherwise. I say this on the basis of our faith which holds that the entire organization of nature, as well as all of our human acts, depend upon divine Providence. Apart from this faith, there is no worship of God. . . . We have spoken more insistently elsewhere against those who teach that God created everything by necessity.

To come to the point, then: if anyone seeks, with a true intention of piety, to understand why the passion and death of

Christ were fitting and seemly, he will discover more and more truths which appear more and more significant the more deeply he contemplates them. In this way, he will experience the truth of the words of the Apostle, who said: "We preach a crucified Christ; to the Jews an obstacle that they cannot get over, to the pagans madness, but to those who have been called, whether they are Jews or Greeks, a Christ Who is the power and wisdom of God." And again: "For God's foolishness is wiser than human wisdom" (1 Cor 1:23-25).

ST. THOMAS AQUINAS, *On the Reasons for the Faith*, Chapter 7.

XII

ETERNAL BEATITUDE[1]

If for any man the tumult of the flesh fell silent, silent the images of the earth, and of the waters, and of the air; silent the heavens; silent for him the very soul itself, and he should pass beyond himself by not thinking upon himself; silent his dreams and all imagined appearances, and every tongue, and every sign; and if all things that come to be through change should become wholly silent to him—for if any man can hear, then all these things say to him, "we did not make ourselves," but He Who endures forever made us—if when they have said these words, they then become silent, for they have raised up his ear to Him Who made them, and God alone speaks, not through such things but through Himself, so that we hear His Word, not uttered by a tongue of flesh, nor by an angel's voice, nor by the sound of thunder, nor by the riddle of a similitude, but by himself whom we love in these things, Himself we hear without their aid—even as we then reached out and in swift thought attained to that eternal Wisdom which abides over all things—if this could be prolonged, and other visions of a far inferior kind could be withdrawn, and this one alone ravish, and absorb, and hide away its beholder within its deepest joys, so that sempiternal life might be such as that moment of understanding for which we sighed, would it not be this:

"Enter into the joy of your Lord?" When shall this be? When "we shall all rise again, but we shall not all be changed."

> ST. AUGUSTINE, *The Confessions of St. Augustine*, Translated with an Introduction and Notes, by John K. Ryan, Doubleday Image Books, New York, 1960, p. 222.

Footnotes

1. Here St. Augustine describes Christian ecstasy such as he experienced just before the death of his mother and companion, St. Monica, at Ostia, near Rome. This ecstasy is precisely that of the blessed who "live with Him in love" (Ws 3:9) while awaiting the final resurrection.

XIII

"I BELIEVE IN THE RESURRECTION OF THE BODY"[1]

We will rise again; we will have bodies that are eternal but they will not be the same. If someone has been just he will be given a celestial body that will fit him to live among the angels. If someone has been a sinner, he will be given an eternal body that will be able to bear the punishment for sin without ever being consumed by the eternal fire. It is fitting that God has so ordained things for both the just and the unjust. We do nothing without our bodies. We blaspheme with our mouths, or we pray with the same mouths. We steal with our hands, or we give alms with the same hands. And so it is with the rest of our bodies. Since the body has in all circumstances been the faithful servant of the soul, it necessarily shares the destiny of the soul.

Let us then take care of our bodies, brothers; let us not abuse them as if they were alien from us. Let us not say, like the heretics, that the body is distinct from the self; let us treat our bodies as a valued property. We must answer to the Lord for everything that has been done by the body. . . .

Traces of sin nevertheless remain in the body. Just as a wound inflicted on the flesh leaves a scar even after it has healed, so the presence of sin affects both the body and the soul; its scars remain in everybody; they are not removed except in those who receive the "bath" [of baptism]. In baptism, God washes away the marks of past sins on both the body and the soul. As for future sins, given our nature, let us fortify ourselves against them so that, keeping pure our fleshly garment, the body, we may not forfeit eternal salvation by any miserable sin such as fornication, sensuality, or any other fault, but rather we may share in God's eternal kingdom for which God Himself deigns to make us worthy by the gift of His own grace.

ST. CYRIL OF JERUSALEM,
Jerusalem Catecheses XIX-XX.

Footnotes

1. St. Cyril of Jerusalem (A.D. 314-387) is addressing adult catechumens in fourth century Jerusalem, just prior to their baptism.

XIV

IDENTITY OF OUR PRESENT BODIES
AND OUR RESURRECTED BODIES

Our resurrection will resemble the resurrection of Christ. As St. Paul wrote to the Philippians (3:2), "He will transfigure these wretched bodies of ours into copies of His glorious body. He will do that by the same power with which He can subdue the whole universe." Now Christ, after His resurrection, possessed a body that could be touched, one made of flesh and bone. According to St. Luke (24:39), He said the following to His disciples after His resurrection: "Touch Me and see for yourselves; a ghost has not flesh and bones as you can see I have." Other men, therefore, when they rise, will have bodies that can be touched, bodies made of flesh and bone . . .

. . . The soul, being identical in species, it seems that it must have matter that is identical in species. After the resurrection the body will therefore be identical with what it was before; it will be made of flesh and bone and of similar elements.

The definition of natural beings which expresses the essence of the species to which they belong includes matter; from this it results that if the matter is affected by a species change, the species of the natural being in question changes also. Now man is a natural being. If, then, after the resurrection, man did not have a body composed of flesh, bone and other similar elements, as is the case with man now, then the being that rose would not belong to the same species, and the term "man" could not even be applied to such a being except in an equivocal sense. . . .

. . . It is wholly impossible to imagine that the body could be transformed into spirit . . . If the body were transformed into the soul, there would no longer be anything but the soul, before or after the resurrection. In this event the resurrection would effect no change in the condition of man. If the body were transformed into another, spiritual substance, the result would be that two spiritual substances would produce a being, one of them by nature, which is impossible because each spiritual substance subsists by itself.

ST. THOMAS AQUINAS, *Summa contra Gentiles*, Book IV, Chapter 84.

APPENDIX OF ILLUSTRATIONS

Relief sculpture from Egina, now in the Athens Museum. Orpheus, shown descending into hell to rescue Eurydice, is a symbol of human survival after death. We see here how Christians depicted Orpheus in the guise of the biblical David, himself a figure of Christ. The animals gathered around him are the pagan nations, invited in the Gospels to believe in the resurrection and rediscover their dignity as children of God.

Jesus Christ the Savior, in the Guise of Orpheus

"The Savior of mankind by means of the human body to which He deigned to unite His divinity, revealed Himself to all as a doer of good in the same way as the Orpheus of the Greeks had. Orpheus tamed and mastered even wild beasts by means of his lyre and of the skill of his handling of them.

"The Greeks, indeed, recounted his prodigies, and believed that the inspired lines of this divine poet not only affected the animals but that even plants and trees were moved to leave their places and follow him by the sound of his voice. Thus it was also with the Savior of mankind; His word was filled with divine wisdom to such an extent that it touched the hearts of men and cured their vices. The human nature He assumed operated in the manner of a sublime Orphic lyre: it charmed, enchanted and ravished, not animals incapable of reason, but rather human creatures possessing the divine gift of a rational soul. Christ in His humanity refined and civilized the crude mores of both the Greeks and the barbarians, and brought under control the most disordered and ferocious passions."

—*EUSEBIUS OF CAESAREA,*
Panegyric of Constantine, Chapter 14.

"Orpheus said to his son Musaeus: 'I sing for the pious, never mind the skeptics . . . ! Formerly you learned from me pernicious doctrines casting doubt upon the reality of a future life; now let me impart to you a wiser teaching. Meditate upon the divine Word; adopt it fully and make it your own. Form your spirit and behavior in the light of this Word. Walk righteously. Adore the king of the universe.'"

—*ANONYMOUS: text probably devised by a Christian*
in order to attract the adherents of an Orphic.

Detail of a sixth-century mosaic in a country house in Daphne, Greece.

According to the ancient legends, the phoenix rose from his own ashes after 500 years. This legend was interpreted by antiquity generally as a symbol of reincarnation; but the Egyptians conceived it as a symbol of the resurrection! For Christians the same decorative motif became, for the same reason, a symbol of Christ, Who rose from the dead by His own power and Who is the principle of the resurrection for all who believe in Him (cf. Jn 11:5-26).

THE OPEN EYES OF THE CRUCIFIED

Fresco from the Church of Santa Maria Antiqua, Rome.

Very ancient representations of the crucifixion show Jesus on the cross with *open eyes*. This type of representation derives from pagan models, as we see in a representation of the tortures of Hesione, the girl rescued from a monster by Heracles. Prometheus too was represented in this fashion. The intention of the artist was to show that Jesus did not go to perdition but, on the contrary, that He was a living and eternal being. In the East, especially in Egypt and Syria, dead persons were often represented with their eyes open in order to demonstrate the inner, spiritual reality of immortality, neglecting the material aspect. The eyes were considered "the mirror of the soul," and the aim was the depiction of the soul. Jesus passed through the ordeal of suffering and death like a conqueror who refused even to lower his eyes.

THE RESURRECTION OF JESUS

Sarcophagus in the Vatican Museum entitled *"Anastasis"* ("Re-surrection") from about 300 A.D.

Primitive Christian art avoided any realistic portrayal of the crucifixion or resurrection of Jesus and limited itself to symbolic representations of these events for a very long time. Thus, in the central panel here, we find summed up the mystery of the death and resurrection of Jesus: at the bottom, there is a cross representing the crucifixion, along with two guards slumbering at the entrance to the tomb; at the top there is a *labarum*, which was the symbol of the victory of the risen Christ, bearing the first two letters in Greek of the word "Christ": KR, *Kristos*. The scenes on each side of the central panel with the *labarum* depict Jesus on the way towards the victory of the cross: the Crowning with Thorns, the Carrying of the Cross, etc.

"Apocalypse," preserved in the municipal library of Trier, Ms. 31, Fol. 67, IXth c.

The Last Judgment and the Resurrection of the Dead go together, as Tertullian explained in his *Apologetics* (Chapter 48). At the bottom, on the left, angels are gathering dispersed bones; also on the left, some resuscitated bodies of the damned follow their chief, Satan; above, the resuscitated just salute Jesus their Savior; at the top, God is presented with books containing the good (left) and the bad (right) works. These good works lead to the heavenly Jerusalem, on God's right hand.

ENOCH AND ELIJAH

Greek Icon, XVII Century, oil painting on wood.

The resurrection of Christ is generally not depicted in Byzantine art in the same fashion as it is commonly depicted in Western art. Christ is not represented as emerging from the tomb; rather he is shown "descending into hell" to rescue the just who lived in the days of the Old Covenant.

Here Jesus leans towards Adam and takes him by His right hand; He takes Eve by His left hand. Adam and Eve are coming out of their tombs. In the opening are seen the gates of hell which Jesus has broken. Two angels lean towards these gates where shades seem to be coming up. Behind Adam and Eve are seen various personages, mostly from the Old Testament: St. John the Baptist, who points out Christ with his finger to Kings David and Solomon, followed by others. Behind Eve there is a second group, at the head of which comes Moses wearing robes resembling those of Christ, Whose coming Moses prophesied; then comes Isaiah. In the cleft of the rocks, four angels hover, one bearing a cross, another a jar of vinegar with a reed and a sponge (instruments of the Passion of Christ). At the extremities of the rocks, forming the gates of hell, are found two men bearing long scrolls: one of these men is *Enoch*, the other *Elijah*. These two were believed not to have tasted death but rather to have been preserved to await the coming of the Anti-Christ in order to do battle with him and be killed by him before Jerusalem. This is an admirable but late echo of the legend holding that Enoch and Elijah would reappear at the end of time.